A List of
"Miracles"
and Daring to Tell

Elizabeth Farrel

BALBOA.
PRESS

A DIVISION OF HAY HOUSE

Balboa Press books may be ordered through booksellers or by contacting:

Balboa Press
A Division of Hay House
1663 Liberty Drive
Bloomington, IN 47403
www.balboapress.com
1-(877) 407-4847

ISBN: 978-1-4525-4353-6 (sc)
ISBN: 978-1-4525-4354-3 (hc)
ISBN: 978-1-4525-4352-9 (e)

Library of Congress Control Number: 2011962051

Printed in the United States of America

Balboa Press rev. date: 12/28/2011

Preface

As a girl of eight I discovered love in nature. Later God became part of that discovery. To the combination of these two has been added a need to express myself. These expressions naturally grew from those sources. I started to draw, paint, write poetry, sing, dance, and create woodcarvings. I made up stories for children spontaneously linked to nature and love, to magic and mystery. This direction has led me through all the experiences, which have propelled me to the writing of this book. My curiosity about the mysteries of nature still draws me like a magnet.

One could say that art, poetry, music and dance, and all creativity, are miracles. I also see love as a miracle, but I am not even writing about those, even though they are common with me. I am speaking of other things, mostly experiences and photographs that were unusual and even amazing to me. Most were surprises. Some however, I asked for, and received. I had that "mustard seed" of faith to make them happen.

The reason that I want to share this information is three-fold. First, I need to do it for my own needs. (I want to keep a record to help me remember and to pass it on to my children and grandchildren). Second, I believe that humanity needs to realize that there are things that are just as real and amazing, even though you can't see them with your mortal eyes, as the things that you *can* see. (Love is one of them!) Also, I want to let you know that you, as a human being, have the power latent within you too, and could potentially see and experience the same types of "miracles". You can make things happen too! Some things I have seen or photographed are simply parts of nature of which we, as humans, have gradually become aware. I want you to experience these kinds of "miracles" and be blessed by them. I want you too to have the "mustard seed" of belief that will make things happen. Thirdly, I want to give credit to God "Mother Nature" and all the invisible forms that help to keep our world afloat. I believe they would be glad that I am sharing my experiences regarding them. I think they wanted me to do so.

I believe there is "magic" out there and wonderful, amazing critters of all kinds in the forms of butterflies, birds and animals, all designed by a Master Designer. Every day I am awed by more of them. These wonders fill up and beautify my world. They make living a magical experience. And being the exceptionally sensitive person I am has its good points. It helps in seeing and being "awake" to them.

A word about the photos: I used a Kodak Easy Share DX7590 digital camera with 5.0 mega pixels and a 10X zoom for all the photos. Some of them have been cropped to show the detail and others left in the more original form to show the location where they were found. Also, the Deva photos look large even though the Devas themselves are tiny, only about 1/8 inch big in most cases.

Some of the photos were taken in a forest in New Hampshire. At the time the sun was in the west behind the trees. My camera was facing downward. I did not use a flash. One of the photos was taken in a forested park along a pond in Haverhill, Massachusetts. No flash was used. There were trees all around. Again, the camera was facing downward. The picture with part of a bridge was taken on a cloudy day. It rained later. I did use a flash. No flash was used however, at my friend's house down the street. Both showed the same type of orb.

I have shared a few of the photos in this writing with several people and they all agree with my conclusions regarding the identity of the types of orbs. Those people are listed in the "Acknowledgements" page.

All poetry in this book is written by myself if not specifically named as another authors' work.

A few last comments: I want you to know that life/nature is really "stranger than fiction" and I am not making up any of the experiences or changing them for effect, nor am I doing this for money. All I have is the truth. I have not changed that. No one could. Believe or not as you see fit.

I love you all who have the ability to believe or are perhaps upon the verge of belief, as you will be given a gift. You have enough love in you to receive it. "In nature are the fingerprints of God".* If you look carefully you may see them.

*Note: Although I have thought in terms of "The Fingerprints of God" as love, joy, and beauty, if you look on the Internet for "The Fingerprints of God" you will see information on the Fabinacci Numbers, which are discussed with awe by many. These numbers are believed to exist in all of the designs of nature and in the universe itself. Many believe it is proof of the "Great Designer" – God. (Sometimes I call Him "The Big Guy".)

Dedication

This book is dedicated to God, Mother Nature and to all her invisible Devas and Nature Spirits who tirelessly continue to do their job in the face of severe adversity. May they never give up on humanity!

Acknowledgements

I would like to thank the special people who have made it possible for me to understand the experiences I have had, and to encourage and help me. The following is a list of these wonderful individuals who have graced my life, taught me about some of these "miracles" and made this book possible: Rev. Carl Franklin, Rev. Ortrun Franklin, Janet Reynolds, Tilley Hagen (author of *The Five Step Process to Escape From Abuse*), who gave me direction, information and solace with their readings. Teri Taylor LGSW, CCDC, gave me wonderful healing Reiki sessions and information along with her support and friendship. I want to thank Ken Ruby, who has been a good listener and friend for 20 years. He saw some of the chapters and said he liked them. Rose Nellett, Mary Hirsch, Ed Leary, Ron Brown, Bill Redding and Jeanette Rowan gave encouragement. Jeanette also helped to edit this manuscript and had the courage to share her own experiences within the pages of this work. Phyllis Brown helped in editing the manuscript for this book also. All of the above listed friends listened to my stories, gave me information, and supported me with their magical friendship.

I also met a man at "Tiller's and Toilers" (which is the common garden in Sun City Center, Florida), who encouraged me to write down my information and experiences having to do with nature. It was this man, who's name I unfortunately cannot remember, who was responsible for the very idea of this book. God bless him. If he finds and reads this book some day, perhaps he will be glad to know what proceeded from his brief conversation with me.

Contents

List of Photographs

CHAPTER ONE

In The Beginning

It amazes me how early the experiences of someone's life can change the direction of it. In my case I was two years old. I don't remember much from that time, but the events affected the rest of my life. It began when I was transported to my grandparent's home and left there for a month or two. My mother was in the hospital giving birth to my sister. (New mothers stayed in the hospital much longer in those days.) It gave me the chance to get to know and love my grandparents.

During my stay with these special people, I became very attached to them, as I could see from a photo I was given of myself with my paternal grandfather at that age. I was hiding in his arms, afraid that someone would take me away from my only safety net. I can still feel that strong connection and that terror. I have re-lived those feelings and know deeply what I must have felt when my parents came to retrieve me. However, I didn't have to guess. My parents told me that I cried in desperation as they tore me out of my grandfather's arms that day. I rarely felt safe anywhere after that. I tried to hide from my family. I hid in closets, and basement hideaways. Once I hid in the woods on my way to school. I eventually, connected the dots, and the picture felt sad but logical.

In spite of being born in Connecticut, I grew up in a little community on the outskirts of Washington, DC, called Silver Spring, MD, which at that time still had a little bit of nature left around it. As a child of eight,

I "escaped" to those areas. I needed to be alone. I finally felt safe there. At first I did not know why I felt better in nature. It was subtle, but it was consistent. It was gentle. It was here that I discovered what love in nature felt like. Nature's love snuck up on me. I could *feel* it. I could not help but love it back. The love I received there may well have saved my life later on, and it certainly has made life bearable in the hard times. It also has added inestimably to my joy. Sometimes I wonder if God gave me this connection to keep me alive.

At ten years old, my father gave me a poetry book for Christmas and I became so engrossed in it that I wanted to write my own poetry. I have been writing poetry ever since. It is a reflection of my soul. I am beginning this by including the following poetry because I feel it is pertinent. It follows the growth of my love of nature. My hope is that this poetry gives the reader a picture of who I was even as a child. My connection to the earth was important to me even then. It set the stage for what came later.

At ten years old, I wrote the following simple poem:

A PLANT

A plant is a wonderful
Thing that grows
When water is sprinkled
At it's toes.

When I was about 17 when I wrote this:

THE LIGHTS OF HEAVEN

In silent reverence I view
The light of the stars
And in that silent sparkling,
I see the lights of heaven.

When I was a teen in the 1960's, the next poem came to me full-blown, inspired by walking in a wild area. The adventure continued! Later, it seemed to me that the cadence of it was like something in the bible, perhaps one of the psalms. I feel it was a forerunner to expressing my deep spirituality.

FOREIGNER
(To those who have yet to see)

I was a foreigner at first, as you are now.
I walked and didn't see
The leaves as they danced in the wind.
I did not hear the birds,
As they sang their songs of joy.
I did not feel the soft breath of the wind
As you do not,
But things have changed with me,
And I know it was me,
For God and His works never change.
I walk in the rain,
And I feel its clean quietness
To my soul's depth.
When the sun shines and the wind sighs,
I feel I must run or die.
Knowledge no longer eludes me.
I have gained an awareness
Of the things which are God's.
When I go someday to answer the call,
And I feel I must,
I will run with a song in my heart
And a joy everlasting.

Later, other poetry came to me as a teen. Here is one. It tells of wanting to share this special love I had found.

A STORY OF GOD

I'll fly to the hills.
I'll run to the sea.
I'll yell it. I'll scream it.
I'll whisper to thee.
A story told by the flowers,
And sung by the gentle rain.
A story in the sunset
And on a winding lane.
A story told by the sunrise
On the shores of a mighty sea,
And all I want for you to do
Is to tell it back to me.

I grew a large collection of poetry on the subject of nature over the years. Here are some I wrote as an adult. I believe that writing my feelings down was helpful to me. Always in the background, however was the solid foundation of love given to me at the age of eight by "my discovery".

LET THE FOREST BE MY HEAVEN

Let the forest be my heaven,
And the sun my only God.
Let the music of the woodlands
Tell you where my feet have trod.
The music and the mystery
The magic and the fire,
Everything I wished for
That was all of my desire . . .
Let no man come between us
For they shall never see
What is was, and what I wished,
And what I came to be.

THE GLORY OF GOD

Thy earth shall speak Thy name to me,
Thy glory fill the skies,
And every tree shall bend in awe.
My spreading soul shall fly.
Upon Thine earth shall peace reign free.
And every bird shall sing.
Upon their knees shall all mankind
Bow before their King.
Could they but know Thy loving heart,
Thy strength when times are bad,
Thine understanding cheerful song
When kindly souls are sad,
They too would sing thy praises Lord,
And know within their heart
The peace and strength that I have known.
A loving God Thou art.

GREAT BEAUTY

Oh, saw I, great beauty then
A'dancing in the trees,
Swaying with the melodies
Of flowers in the breeze.
In the majesty of morning,
Reflections in the sky,
In shady nooks and puddles,
The earth would make me cry.
The singing birds, the misty rose,
Are filled with love for me,
The lonely walks and little talks,
God nudging me to see.

CHAPTER TWO

Meeting God / Heavenly Music

How does someone "meet God" for the first time? Well, I would bet it is different for each person. But this is my story. For me it was in stages.

I guess we are all made aware some time in our lives that there are people who go to church and that those who do generally believe in God. My parents did not, and they did not go to church, but they wanted me to see if I liked it – as an educational experience. I did not have a real opinion. I was very young and I was with only strangers. I did not care very much about it. I was only five years old.

When I was about eight years old I started to spend time away from my family. I would go to a little bit of wooded land that surrounded our little neighborhood. It felt so good to be alone out there that I continued to visit the area. It *felt* friendly. It made me feel stronger and more important somehow. I wondered what it was that made me feel that way. I found out that nature could give me a very good feeling and I decided it was love. Later I heard that Love equaled God. Some say in fact that it is God's "Name".

Then came a time that I was in terrible physical pain and I asked to the air – God if you do exist, please take my pain away. It didn't happen right away – but looking back now, I know that the same periodic pain

I was having was taken away. My mother finally brought me to a doctor who gave me medication.

Next, began a series of "coincidences". I became involved in a church and sang in a choir due to a friend's insistence that I join her as a choir member. I was in the sixth grade. Afew years later I joined the MYF (Methodist Youth Fellowship), and eventually was able to go on a "retreat" for a week. I was 17. I loved singing at each meal, sharing a room with a kind young lady and telling stories etc. I shared my poetry and heard jokes… and … "met God in Western Maryland". I was sorry to have to go home. I loved those people. I felt safe.

On the way home from this event, I shared a ride with several other teens. One of the mothers drove us back. During that ride in the car, I sat in the back seat. I remembered how beautiful the recent experience was and how I was inspired by the last song. I felt changed somehow. I could hear the sounds of the tires on the road and the wind coming in the windows. Then I began to hear something else. It sounded like a large group of people singing in harmony. I could not make out the words. They seemed to be singing in an unknown language. For some reason it sounded strangely like angels singing. It was quite beautiful. The song lasted about 15 minutes. I don't believe anyone else heard anything. I was afraid to tell anyone, but I truly believed in my heart that angels were making that music.

About 40 plus years later I was able to see a very special man for a "reading", Carl Franklin, who had been a minister, a psychologist and a speaker on the metaphysical scene. He could tell me the truth about what I experienced. He has the ability to see "beyond the veil". He told me "absolutely" that "The angels were celebrating" what just happened in my life. Since that time Carl has been pivotal in my spiritual growth and therefore will be mentioned several times in this writing.

When I returned from the "retreat" I planned to discuss the idea becoming a Minister. The next time I attended church I planned to speak to the Minister, but the minute I walked into the church I heard him ask for any *boys* that might consider the ministry to join him later to discuss it. It was the first time I had heard that call, (then only for males) since I started going to that church. It seemed obvious that women were not wanted in that field. I did not pursue it. (Later on in my life I told God I was thinking about being a minister and I got back a response of "Oh, my dear child!".

THERE ARE TIMES

There are times
When the world
Is a crystal flower
That only I can see.
And sometimes
The wind is a
Beloved friend
That speaks to me.

CHAPTER THREE

Sligo Creek Park

I.
BELONGING

Perhaps it was in 1960, but I can no longer remember the exact year that this experience occurred. I do remember the feeling of awe. I was still living at home with my parents and had gotten into the habit of going for walks in the park. It was about a ten- minute walk to get to Sligo Creek Park from my home in Silver Spring, Maryland. I loved being there, and when I could manage it, I would ride my bike to the park. I went there most often alone, although I had been warned not to do so by my mother. She was afraid of what might happen to me (although she never really explained what that entailed). I simply watched very carefully – especially males. If I saw a man, I would get out of there fast and/or hide until I felt safe.

On one particular day, I had walked to the park and "soaked up" the atmosphere. I remember that I started to "create" a song that came to me out of the blue. It came to me word-by- word and its verses rhymed. I thought it was beautiful. I did not have any way to write it down and I forgot it almost immediately. I felt sad that it just disappeared into the nothingness from which it came.

I walked on and came to an area with more vegetation where I would not be seen. This made me happy. I had begun to feel "different" from the time I was "given" the song, and somehow the feeling of being "different" intensified. I began to identify the feeling as "being *part* of nature" as though I was not human any longer. I "belonged" there. I saw a group of bees at that point, which would ordinarily make me walk the other way since I was usually terrified of them. That day, and that moment, I was not. It surprised me. I somehow "knew" that I was part of nature and that the bees also felt it. I "knew" they would not hurt me. I stayed as long as I could to enjoy this amazing sensation, then I walked home. When I arrived at home the "magic" was gone. Maybe someday I can recreate that experience. That is my wish.

II.
EDEN

On another adventure hike to Sligo Creek Park, I followed the stream, walking further into the park. I stopped to scan the area and noticed a grove of trees that I had seen before, but that area looked somehow very different. It was not just because of the flowers growing there, which were lovely purple and white violets, or the way the sunshine streamed down. This time it seemed "magical". I couldn't keep my eyes off it. I tried to come up with a way to describe it. Two ways kept coming to mind. One was that I was looking at "Eden", that beautiful garden described in the bible. The other word that came to mind was "Heaven". Either way I felt that God was giving me the gift of a lifetime. It was hard to leave. Somehow I felt I might never see it again.

QUIET PLACES

In quiet places the sunlight roars
And dances as it dips and soars
About the violets newly grown
And the grasses newly sewn.
You'd think it was a'rollicking
For some fun and frolicking,
But then I know it's wise to see
That God is there and watching me.

CHAPTER FOUR

Christened by God

When I lived at home with my parents, I was constantly looking for places to be alone with nature. I combed the neighborhood for appropriate hidden areas that could meet my needs and found several. One summer day in my teens, I decided to go to one of those special places to be alone with God.

Singing in the choir at a local Methodist church kept reminding me about God on a regular basis. As I remember it, I had been to church that day. I had a good experience there. I was still thinking about that as I walked through the neighborhood to an area at the end of a row of houses, where the area was wild. I walked up to a hilltop that was on the edge of the highway, but surrounded by trees. As usual I soaked in the beauty of the place and enjoyed the presence of God.

The longer I was there, the better I felt. I thought of ways to be kind to my family. I felt loving. I was having one of the best days I could recall at that location. I was noticing the details of the setting. The dew on leaves of a tree near me, shown in the sunlight. I walked closer and stared at it. I saw the reflections of the sky and the colors of the leaves in the dew. The delicate beauty of it filled me with joy and I was very grateful for that gift. I was awed.

Suddenly something told me that God was in that dew looking back at me. I was "blown away" by strong feelings that it was *real*. It was a new idea for me, but I believed it. It also made sense to me and I felt honored.

Then it started to rain very gently. I thought of how often people would go to church and be christened or baptized and I had a strong feeling that due to my experience with God on that day, He had decided to accomplish this directly with this rain. I felt it and was awed by it. I thanked Him with all my heart.

After a while I knew I would have to go back home. I was getting wet. I didn't really want to interfere with "The Christening" so I walked slowly on my way down the hill and back around the neighborhood towards home. I walked in wonder.

I was almost home when one of my neighbors, who happened to be outside on her porch, noticed me walking by. She called to me, and when I turned around she told me about how she thought I might get sick from being out in the rain and offered to bring me an umbrella. I thanked her for her kindness, but told her I knew I would be fine and she didn't need to worry. I didn't say any more. I did not want to tell her why. I knew she would not believe me. To me it would be illogical for God to allow me to get ill due to a blessing of His own design. God doesn't work like that. I did not become ill.

Many years later, after I moved away and became a wife and a mother, etc., I went to another church. After I had sung in their choir for about 20 years, the Minister suggested that I get baptized. I told him that I had been christened as a baby, which was true. He still thought I should get baptized anyway as an adult, now that I could understand the significance. At that point I felt that I was going to have to tell him my story about The Christening those many years ago in the rain when I lived in Maryland. I knew that he would probably think I had "gone off the edge", but I didn't know what else to tell him but the truth. Whether that is bravery or stupidity is anybody's guess. However, I told him briefly that God had handled that one by Himself many years ago. He stared at me with a look of incredulity and did not press the issue.

Eventually in my life I have learned that my "gut feelings" have turned out to be true. I have learned to trust them.

CHAPTER FIVE

Special Visitor

This story is about something that changed my life. It happened when I was 17, after I heard the angels sing. Suddenly things were going surprisingly well. I was grateful beyond words.

The story begins in a house in Connecticut. It was in a little town called Old Lyme. My sister and I were visiting our favorite aunt and uncle for the summer. We slept in a room on the second floor of their home. My sister had gone to sleep early and I got up and went to the window to pray. It was starting to rain, and during this experience it grew into a thunderstorm.

I had been thinking about all the special things that had started happening to me. I was thanking God for all the wonderful gifts, and good friends that just seemed to appear out of nowhere. I even found, what I felt, was the love of my life. I was so enormously grateful, it was hard to find the words, and I started to cry as I spoke to the God I had grown to love dearer than any human I had ever known. Tears were streaming down my face as I explained to God who "really knew", how I felt.

At that point I felt something, *a power*, come into the room through the window, which was open about six inches. I did not see this energy, but I could feel the power of it profoundly. It felt larger and stronger than my mind could conceive. Something inside me knew without doubt that God had heard me and had come to me. The power of it did more than fill the room. It seemed to fill the whole neighborhood or more…I remember feeling like an ant in the presence of an elephant. In the presence of this "Consciousness" I felt waves of totally encompassing awe.

I began to feel that I didn't deserve such a visit. I was totally overwhelmed. There was nothing but this *Presence* for quite some time. Down on my knees at that point, I tearfully thanked God and bowed my head and held my hands together in prayer. Eventually, I felt that maybe I should get down lower. I lay face down on the floor. I didn't know what to do next. I was so tired from all the emotions. I eventually decided to tell this presence/God that I was incredibly honored, and that It/He didn't really need to stay any longer, as this was enough to last the rest of my life. I meant it. God stayed anyway.

After what seemed a very long time I decided to go back to bed. It was getting uncomfortable on the floor. When I got in bed and lay down next to my sleeping sister, God was still there. I wondered how long He would stay. I didn't know what to do and I was feeling nervous, again, I felt I didn't deserve such an impressive visit. Then my sister woke up and she asked me "Is there someone else in the room?" In a very small shaky voice I said "um … yes, there is". We didn't say much after that and a few minutes later; God "The Power" left the room.

Due to that experience, I became very sure God knew who I was! On top of that, He must *like* me! I felt I met Him "big time". I think it was the gratefulness. That is what was going on when it began. Then the "Coincidences" began.

THERE IS NO NIGHT

There is no night
Without a light,
No desert
Without a flower.

CHAPTER SIX

Message From God

Again, this event also happened when I was seventeen. It was a banner year for the unusual. After that last event some other things happened that seemed to be coincidences at first. They came so fast and kept on coming that I finally had to admit it was getting obvious that they were *not* coincidences. I can't remember some of them any longer, and some were small things to me, but I remember thinking that God was trying very hard to get my attention. And since I felt a bit overwhelmed the last time God showed up at my home (because I couldn't imagine deserving it), maybe He decided to take another tack.

At this point I felt as though God was talking to me through my mind… He would tell me things like "Go outside". And I would do it. Then something nice would happen to me. I was getting used to it. (Now, I notice that this "voice" seems to come from the right side of my head. From my research I found that the right side is the spiritual, artistic, creative side of the brain. To me, it is a logical choice for God to use it.)

It was at this point that my new "boyfriend" came to visit my home and stayed for about a week. (He slept in my brother's room, not mine.) Nothing unusual happened for several days. However, it was not going to stay that way. "Someone" must have had other plans.

There was one day that was warm and we decided to go out on the front porch. I followed him. At that point I got a message from what I knew to be God. I was told to hug him. Well, I always tried to do what God wanted, so I hugged this young man. I got such an amazed look that I couldn't help but ask what was going on. He could hardly speak. It seemed hard to find his voice. Then he asked me why I did it. I didn't want to tell him because it would seem too "weird". Other people don't often get those kinds of messages – do they? It seemed like I better be honest though, because God would not like a lie. So, I gathered my courage and said to him that he would not believe me if I told him the truth, but I would still try it. I told him "God told me to do it".

Well, that about knocked the wind out of my boyfriend. He told me in a shaky voice after a pause, that he had just asked God in a prayer - if He were there, would He "show it through Betsy somehow?" (Betsy was my nickname.) That is when I hugged him.

BIRD IN FLIGHT

Come sail with me upon the wind
Through sunsets, clouds, and bluest skies.
We'll dip and soar upon the breeze,
And dash through leaves on yonder trees,
Over mountains in the sun,
And quiet lakes – we'll have some fun!
Our cries of joy will fill the sky,
Because with me, your soul can fly.

CHAPTER SEVEN

Dental Assistance / Pain Management

Visiting my dentist is not one of my favorite things to do, probably not yours either. Sometimes we just have to do it anyway. Well, this time the dentist told me I needed a crown. (Not a happy thought!) He said he would prepare the tooth that day, and I should come back in a week to complete the process. He started preparing the tooth for the crown. I had to have Novocain. You probably know how I felt when I left. I couldn't feel my mouth. I could barely smile. Then it started to hurt. That was the beginning of a long week of pain. It didn't go away so I started to take Advil. I took it every four hours for most of that week and started to feel that it was not a good idea to take it for so long. I thought I should call my dentist and discuss the problem. I was about to lift the phone when I realized his office was closed on Fridays. I would not be able to see him till Monday. That was not acceptable to me. I figured I had a problem. Something was wrong. Who was there to help me?

Suddenly, I knew the answer - God. I figured that God still liked me and I knew that He knew who I was. Why wouldn't He want to help! Of course He would! Well, I had a "great idea". I would picture Him as a ball of light right next to me. Then I would picture Him coming into my face and into the tooth with the pain. If God was there, surely no bad could be there at the same time. I could just see the ball of light in my mind's eye. So I attempted to get God's attention. Then I told him of my plan. I asked for His help, and then pictured the light coming toward me and going into my mouth to the tooth. *The pain stopped instantly.*

When I finally returned to my dentist, he asked me how I was doing. I told him that I had a problem during the week and solved it myself. He became curious and asked me to explain. I told him I didn't think he would believe me. He said he just might. So I told him the story. He surprised me by telling me that others had told similar stories. He actually believed me!

It was the old "mustard seed" of belief that saved the day. With these "miracles" happening, I guess it doesn't surprise me that I often wax poetic…

LET ME SING

Let me sing my song on a lonely hill
Where the breeze can whisper what I love still,
And the sun can rush with joy to earth,
And I can feel what life is worth.
Let me dance in a meadow of yellow and green,
And feel all the love I've seen.
Again I'll know the joys I've found.
My song will be a happy sound.

CHAPTER EIGHT

Stop The Rain

Many years went by, I married the boyfriend that visited me at my home in my previous story, and had two children. I also ended up divorced after 15 years. (Sometimes things don't work as you plan).

After the divorce things got rather difficult for my children and me. I had to go to work, and I had to worry about money for a change. It was a long time before I got any vacation. However, I had an aunt who lived two hours away at a cottage on a lake. She always welcomed my children and me to visit anytime. Our "vacation" was to visit her for the weekend. I had it all planned.

We had a large yard in those days and it took two days for me to mow it. I was going to have to mow it before I left for the weekend or it would grow too long to cut by the next weekend. We would not be able to go on vacation. So, the day before we were going to take off for the cottage, I started the riding mower and mowed the front yard. I worked on the side yard next and was on the way to the back when I knew there was going to be trouble. It started raining. Normally this would just be an annoyance, but this time it was totally unacceptable to me. This would not do! I needed some help from the "Big Guy"!

I had a one-way conversation explaining the predicament to God. I told Him that I just *had* to finish mowing the yard! Could He at least postpone this rain business? He could start it again after I was done, couldn't He? If the world really needed it, it could still be done. I also wanted to explain how much we needed to go to visit my favorite aunt for the weekend. The divorce had been extremely difficult on my children and me. I said I had been so good that surely He would do this for us. The more I talked, the more I believed God would help me. In that moment of being truly *sure, the rain stopped.* As they used to say in my generation – "I kid you not". I finished mowing the yard and was on my way to the garage when it *started raining* again! I was awed. It felt great. I wanted to dance for joy.

IN A DREAM

In sunlight I was dancing free.
In dreams I whirled in childish glee
A'mid the flowers on a mountain top
And didn't ever want to stop.

No pain or hunger did I know.
I only watched the flowers grow.
I saw my God's delightful day.
The wind blew all my cares away.

T'is sad to know, t'is but a dream,
Oh, so real did it seem,
To be so very happy then.
I hope that it will come again.

CHAPTER NINE

Mount Major, The Love of a Mountain

Having a high level of sensitivity has its drawbacks. One of those is that I have suffered from depression for many years. One day many years ago, it was especially severe and I lay on my bed wondering if there was anything in the world that could make me happy. I had been divorced recently. It had been very difficult to adjust and I had no family living near me.

I lay on my bed fifteen minutes searching my mind for *something* that would propel me out of the suffering. Eventually, I realized that spending time in the woods somewhere safe would feel good to me. I could only think of one safe place. That was a mountain I had been to once before with my husband. It was about an hour and a quarter north on the edge of the White Mountains. I would find it.

Shortly afterward, I found myself on the road to "happiness". When I finally parked in the parking lot below Mt. Major, I knew that I had some serious climbing to do, but I was determined. I did not remember much about the trail, but I would not be deterred. I finally made it up to about half way. In front of me was an area where, if I climbed up a rock wall at a serious angle I could see out, which I did. When I reached that point, I turned around. I gave a surprised cry. The view amazed me. I suddenly started to sob and sat down sharply. I was shocked and awed by the beauty. I felt that I did not deserve the splendor that was laid out before me.

I could see for miles the view of almost all of the 25 miles of Lake Winnipesaukee, and the surrounding mountains and hills all stretched out before me. In the misty distance I could make out the snow covered peak of Mt. Washington. I believed at that moment that this was an awesome gift from God to me personally. I was "blown away" with emotion. It took several minutes to get my bearings and calm down. I stayed there as long as it took to soak up the joy and blessings needed for my healing. By the time I arrived back home I was a "new" woman.

Since then, I have spent many amazing days climbing, wandering, sleeping on the rocks, picking blueberries, and discovering many lovely places on that mountain, until a friend of mine called me the "Queen of the Mountain".

One summer, I spent almost every Saturday up on that mountain. It felt *holy*. I never saw any poison ivy or any kind of danger. I sensed God up there. I could *feel* Him, especially at the summit. Each time I left that mountain, I looked forward with great anticipation to my return. It was like visiting a holy place of God. I sensed God's loving presence like an enormous invisible cloud hovering over the whole top of the mountain.

On other visits to that mountain, I would lie down on one of the huge, flat, secluded rocks and sleep for a while. When I awoke, I felt wonderfully rested and filled with delight.

One winter I wandered around the lower part of the mountain and discovered a group of big boulders in a semi circle. I slept against one of them, facing away from the trail so that no one would find me. I felt safe there with my furry coat around me, lying in a pile of leaves smelling of the earth. I could hear the wind gently blowing through the trees and I breathed the crisp, fragrant air. Again, I felt blessed and contented when I awoke.

On my adventures at Mt. Major I had picnics on what I called my "Lunch Rock". It was half of a round boulder that had broken. This four-foot in diameter boulder was located over the top of the mountain, past the old remains of a "block house". The flat side was facing skyward. It functioned as a table. God seemed to have a way of providing for me.

I had names for other rocks and areas on the trail. For example: The Cathedral, The Bathroom, the Arrow Rock, The Heart Rock, and The Lounge. When I saw them, I felt I was visiting old friends. A smile would suddenly grow on my face and my eyes would "light up".

Sometimes I would bring my friends and show them the way to the top. I would share all the names of my special places and have a picnic on the "Lunch Rock". They seemed to enjoy themselves too.

One day in the winter I decided to drive up and see the mountain. I watched as it began to snow with big, gentle, quiet flakes. The result reminded me of some kind of "fairy land". The snow covered the branches and sides of the trees. It was peaceful and quiet as a church. Both the woods and I were transformed. Tranquility reigned in the quiet beauty and the peace.

Over the many years of visiting this haven, I was inspired to write poetry about the mountain. I could not be still. See below.

THE MAGIC OF THE MOUNTAIN

Upon the friends
Some turned to stare,
(God smiled on those
Who traveled there),
And reaching the summit
It came to be,
They saw the mountains
Reach out to the sea -
Mountains in robes

Of light like queens,
Or hugging the night
Mid stars and dreams.
The magic was made
Like wonder unknown.
The spell was cast
By God alone.
God smiled on those
Who came to share,
And blessed all those
Who traveled there.

THE GIVING OF LOVE

In the distant mountains
On the side of a hill,
Where the sunshine comes
So soft and still,
It lays on the edges
Of uncurling leaves,
And moves about
In the softest breeze.
T'is the gentle magic
Of God's own touch,
That makes the world breathe
That he loves so much.
It's the giving of life,
And His touch of joy
That makes the world
Like a newborn toy.

COME TO THE MOUNTAIN

I know a place where injured souls
are healed by God,
Where beauty and wonder are free,

Where no one wants a thing of me.
A secret place no one else knows,
Where I can simply be . . .
To watch the clouds go sailing by,
Glorious trees against the sky.
Come with me and we will watch
Birds a flyin' far across
Glorious sunsets o're mountains high,
Reaching out to meet the sea.
A perfect place God made for me.
A magic place near sun and sky
Where songs begin and souls must fly.

A SIMPLE SIGH

Through curling mist
The sunshine kissed
My face in love so soft.
The gentle wind
Caressed my skin
Till cares took flight aloft.
The mountain called
My name the same
As years of youth gone by,
Till all the sorrows
Tears and fears
Became a simple sigh.

CHAPTER TEN

Close Call

In 1985, I found myself in need of employment. I had almost no experience and decided the fastest way was to be a Secretary. I signed up with a temporary service. After training, for which I will be eternally grateful, I was sent to Digital Equipment Corporation. One of the many sites I experienced was about an hour from my home. I arose at 5:30am in order to be out on the highway by 7am.

One winter morning, I was on the six-lane highway on the way to work, and it started to snow. They were only gentle flakes and I didn't think it was a "big deal". However, the other cars started to slow down. Apparently they were taking this seriously. I decided to slow down also. I always leave a good distance between my vehicle and the car ahead of me. It came in handy that day. When I stepped on the break nothing happened. I was not immediately frightened since I had left plenty of room. I stepped on the break again and the car still did not respond. Now it started to bother me. I tried again and again with no response. Then I tried another tack. I turned the steering wheel. No response occurred with that action either. Then I became very frightened. I was getting close to the car in front of me at that point. I remember thinking "So this is how I am going to die". My car came to about six feet from the car ahead when my car suddenly swung around to the right and stopped. I was facing the oncoming traffic. I was into a feeling of shock and amazement, but I still had a problem. I could not control the car. The car continued to swirl around again. Eventually, when the car stopped,

I was facing the oncoming traffic, but I was *off the road* against an embankment.

When I had been shaking from fear, shock and amazement for a few minutes, I thought to myself "God still loves me". Later, it went through my mind that " I did not do any of this." Who saved my life?

I checked that stretch of road in the week following this experience, and found that the "important embankment" was the only one on the whole stretch of highway that I had to traverse on my way to work. I no longer could believe this was a coincidence.

I believe, at this juncture, that the Angels saved me. It was not my time to go. There was important work left to do in this lifetime. Additionally, in the years before my divorce, I had begged God to be taken Home, but was not given the chance then either.

When we think all is lost, sometimes we forget that God loves us. Even in the "winter" of our lives, spring is waiting. Nature knows.

FORSYTHIA DREAMS

When cold and snow
Seem to cover the earth,
The forsythia dreams
Of a coming birth.
When the wind is warm,
And the earth is kind,
And the bluebird sings -
Sweet peace of mind.

CHAPTER ELEVEN

Lost Luggage

After my children "left the nest", I started to take some trips by plane. In this case, I went to Florida to visit my parents. It was Christmas. The airline industry seemed to be "all in a flutter" during this time of year. But I managed to get to my destination without any disasters. Honestly, not too much had gone wrong on the other flights I had taken. However, I guess I must have been overdue for a taste of the imperfections of the system. It just hadn't shown up yet.

On my way home, the plane ride seemed more or less normal. I was happily settled into reading a good book unknowingly confident that all would be fine. It was not.

The plane arrived in Boston. My fellow passengers and I stretched our legs and started down to take possession of our luggage. We followed one another like innocent sheep to the appropriate area. As we moved down the stairs I looked for a sign indicating our flight arrival time. However, when I found it, the appropriate sign did not mention that the flight arrived.

The line to get our luggage grew like a giant spring around the room due to my fellow passengers and the addition of those from the other flights whose travelers had the same predicament. No information was available to any of us. I became very concerned. The friend, who came to retrieve me, was unable to wait any longer. I attempted making a phone call to the airline, but had no luck. I wondered if I would ever see my luggage again. Still no sign indicated that we arrived. The rest of the unhappy crowd waited. I walked away.

The weekend came and went. I was very worried about the missing luggage. There were a number of irreplaceable things in my suitcase. Again, this was a time to talk to the "Big Guy". I told Him the situation, and that I had some spiritual/religious music CDs in my luggage that could not be replaced, which were helping me to be in contact with Him. Surely He would want me to have those back. And sure, I wanted my clothing, but I could somehow deal with that loss if I really had to. I felt pretty sure that God would intervene to get me those tapes.

Shortly afterward, a friend volunteered to drive me back to the airport in Boston to see if my luggage appeared. I took him up on it. At least I might get a chance to inquire about what happened to it.

On the Monday after the "Luggage Mystery", I got in my friend's car and we headed to the airport. The closer I got to the airport, the more certain I was that I would find my luggage. I could "feel" it. Upon arrival, we went straight to the luggage area. That huge room was filled almost to the rafters with luggage, and no one was watching it. It was a daunting sight. However, as I was armed with my belief in God, I did not give up. I started scanning the room. To my delight I found my luggage very quickly. This was one of the golden moments that may seem like a coincidence, but was not one to me. I thought "that mustard seed" keeps showing up. Truly God does seem to work in mysterious ways. I was in joy.

A SONG IN THE WIND

I wish to run
As the day grows nigh
Through every meadow
With grass that is high
And waves with a song in the wind.

CHAPTER TWELVE

Who's Calling My Name?

I.
AT DIGITAL EQUIPMENT CORPORATION

As I mentioned earlier, I was working for Digital Equipment Corporation as a Temporary Administrative Assistant for a while, this time in a peaceful area of a building in Massachusetts where I saw very few people during the day.

One day at work, when I seemed to be alone, I was walking to my desk and I heard a voice calling my old nickname, Betsy. I looked around, but saw no one. After I peaked into the "big boss's" office, I realized that in that facility no one knew me by that name. They called me Elizabeth. I was totally perplexed.

Then I tried to figure out what could have happened. At that point, the only thing I could think of was that it could be my grandfather, who had passed on several years before. I had begun to suspect that his spirit was with me in my home. As I mentioned earlier, I had a very loving relationship with him as a child. I thought he might well want to watch over me. In addition, at home there were some strange things happening. My children complained that doors were closing by themselves etc. So when my nickname was spoken at work I could think of no one else who could be responsible for this experience.

II.
A PARKING LOT IN FLORIDA

Years later, I went to live in Florida. A local Lawyer hired me as part-time help. One day, when I was the last to leave my place of work, I went out the door and walked across the empty parking lot to my car. I heard my nickname called again –"Betsy", from behind me. There was only one person in this new community who knew me by that name. I carefully searched the parking lot, but I did not see him, or anyone. To this day I do not know who tried to get my attention. I thought it was a man. Perhaps it could have been my deceased grandfather again? In my heart I believe it was him or even my father who had recently passed away.

III.
AT HOME IN FLORIDA

Also in Florida, a man and his wife hired me to help with their computer and to manage their bank account information on Quicken. The gentleman was a real "sweetheart" of a guy. He reminded me of my deceased father. I was very fond of him. Unfortunately, a year after I was hired, the gentleman died. I was at the hospital attempting to visit him during that very moment he was fighting for his life, and lost.

His death was a great loss for me, as he had been kind to me and a good role model. (He never said an unkind word about anyone.) A few days later, when I was home, I was crying because I loved and missed him. I got up and starting walking into another room. That is when I heard a voice calling out my name – "Elizabeth". He knew me by that name. I was certain that he was the one who said it. I lived alone.

WE ARE NOT ALONE

We are not alone.
Love follows our footsteps . . .
In joy and in sorrows -
Through all our tomorrows.

CHAPTER THIRTEEN

Mystical Slide Show

Being an artist has been one of my joys in life. I began this quest to express my love of nature when I was about eight or ten years old. I wanted to learn how to paint and draw.

At college I became an Art Major. At one point, my teacher told me that I could be "another Rembrandt". When I left college, I remembered that comment, and in its wake, I painted and sold many pictures.

Years later I was asked by my church to paint a mural of a rainbow for their Rainbow Nursery School. I had never created a mural before, but decided to embark upon this new adventure. Upon completion, the people at the church were happy. Additionally, the experience had now given me the chance to discover how to find the paint colors and other equipment I would need. Later I painted murals for family and friends.

Things blossomed and the word got out about my murals. I received a call from a lady at White Pines College to do a "One Man Show". After participating in that show, a reporter from one of the local newspapers interviewed me. During the interview the woman took my photo while I painted a mural at my home. Shortly afterward my picture appeared in a local paper, which produced a customer for my work, a lady from a nearby town who saw the article. She decided to hire me to paint a mural in her basement. I agreed.

I attempted to do a preliminary painting to show her the plan. The exact color green for the grass eluded me. I mixed all versions of green and could not seem to get it right. Then I remembered that this painting was for a lovely lady who wanted very much to show her children the memories of what a happy life they led while the children were growing up in that house. I wanted to give her that. I thought it was something that God would bless. So, since I was now getting used to the idea of asking for God's help, I called on Him again.

After putting in the plea for this woman to have what she wanted, I lay down on my bed and closed my eyes. In a few minutes, to my surprise, I began to see, what I now label, a "mystical slide show" of beautiful natural areas. In living color I saw the grass I had wanted to see. I saw a meadow with apple trees growing in it and tree branches against the sky. The scenes looked real enough to touch. The wind was blowing the leaves. The scenes would come sliding in from the right and stop for a minute and continue going off to the left. Then a warm blackness would cross my vision till the next beautiful view arrived. This "show" lasted about five or ten minutes. I had tears in my eyes when it stopped. I was grateful for having God as a partner in my life. I felt blessed. The color of the grass was perfect and I used it.

I'M IN LOVE

I'm in love. I'm in love with the grass and the trees,
With the clouds and the flowers, the birds and the bees,
With mountains and meadows, the moon and the sun,
The seas and the oceans and rivers that run.

I'm in love. I'm in love with the flowers that bloom,
With the frogs and the turtles and the sun in my room,
With the dawn and the sunsets, reflections of love
In the eyes of a child of our God above.

I'm in love. I'm in love with the stars that shine,
The minnows and whales and dew on the vine,
With the mist on the ponds and the wind in my hair,
And the joy of just knowing that our God is there.

CHAPTER FOURTEEN

Visions

I.
THE WHITE YACHT

In the experience I am about to discuss, I was awake with my eyes closed. I don't know if you ever saw anything in that state. And I don't remember seeing things in my youth when I closed my eyes, but sometimes I do now. Some call it meditation. Sometimes it hasn't brought me anything that seems useful, but I get surprises. In the last chapter, I told about the slideshow, which is related to this type of event. Here are more experiences, some of them a little different.

A few years ago I decided to go to a class in meditation. It has always been a difficult thing for me to meditate for more than a few seconds and I thought I needed some help. After I had gone to the weekly meetings for a while, I had a lovely experience.

As the group became silent and closed their eyes to meditate, I closed mine and went into the darkened silence. After remembering the slide show that I had been given previously, I knew to look in the same way. I soon became aware of "being" near a little lake and looking across to the reflections in the water. There were trees near the edge. Everything was in color and it felt real. I was "there". It felt peaceful and lovely. The water was moving in gentle waves to the shore. After staring at this scene for a while, off to the right appeared a beautiful, pure white yacht sailing slowly into my view. I couldn't keep my eyes off it. After the yacht was in full view, the vision was gone.

When the group came out of their own meditations, I asked what they thought this vision meant. I was told that the yacht symbolized my soul.

II.
VISITORS

In the first "reading" by Carl Franklin I was given some information, which related to what angels, guides etc. were part of the personal team "assigned" to me to watch over and help me in this life. I was also told there may be others "from beyond the veil". When I heard this I was curious who they were. I prayed one night to have them come to me in a dream so I could know who they were. It seems that I was heard. I had dreams that night. First, I saw six boys that I thought had been mine in a previous life. I saw them as small children playing in a shallow pond, then as young men. At that point I danced with them. Then my maternal grandmother showed up and I danced with her also. I told "the boys" that she was the one who had taught us to dance. We should thank her. The applause for her was heartfelt. She smiled and walked away.

I believe the next event was a response to that same request as well, but I am not sure if I was actually asleep, awake or having another type of experience.

I was lying on my bed one day. I assume my eyes were closed, but I am not sure. Suddenly I saw two "people" in my room. The first was at the foot of my bed. I sensed this was a female. She was a white, very indistinct short spirit. She suddenly seemed to notice that I saw her and she got very excited and happy. She immediately "flew" towards me in great joy. I could feel that she wanted to hug me. I could tell she must be someone that loved me and that I had known her before. She disappeared when she was about two inches from my face. I felt a terrible loss when she was gone. I still wonder about her identity. However, my mother had passed on a few years before and she was about that size. I remember thinking of her at that moment. The vision was too indistinct to be sure, but if my "gut instinct" is right, and am learning more and more to trust it, she was the one who joyfully tried to hug me.

In the wake of that experience, I looked toward my bedroom door. There was a tall thin man standing there with brown hair down to his shoulders. I wondered if he was Jesus. I was not afraid of him. He came towards me and I got the feeling he intended to kiss me on the cheek. When he reached me, he disappeared as though he went through me. This was much like the last experience with the female spirit. Since Jesus has been described as a Master, and since I was told I had one assigned to me, I expected that he was the one I saw. (Not long afterwards, I learned to use a pendulum to ask questions of my personal team of light workers and guides. I asked then if Jesus had appeared to me in that instance. The answer was yes.)

Next, two older gentlemen, with some gray in their hair, showed up and each took a turn coming to me and disappearing when they got really close. They both wore colorful short-sleeved shirts with designs on them. If my memory serves me, one had pictures of boats on his shirt. It felt like they were introducing themselves to me. Since I had put in a "request" for my personal team of guides and others to show themselves, and since this experience occurred soon after that, I now believe the last two were probably my "Spirit Guides". I was told that I had three.

III.
A NEW HOUSE

Sometimes when I meditate, I see visions. This time I was listening to a CD, which told me to imagine an Angel and hold his hand. This meditation was supposed to show me my life one year in the future. I was to follow this Angel. I closed my eyes and during this exercise, I actually walked around my bed a short distance while as I imagined myself following the Angel. I pictured a dark corridor leading down into the earth. At the end I saw a doorway. I walked to that doorway and looked out observing a backyard with a lovely setting and a man clipping bushes in the yard. The man appeared to be about my age with wavy thin blond hair. There were low growing colorful flowers next to the house and a hedge around a patio made with flat stones about three inches by three inches. There was an arbor at an exit point across from me. Also in the yard there was a picnic bench and a rock fireplace on which to cook. There were large trees just outside the patio. No houses were in view. This was all in living color, with great detail and movement.

When I opened my eyes I was back in my bedroom. Since this was showing me one year into my future, I knew that it was telling me I would be in a setting like the one I was shown. I felt very much encouraged by this experience. I prayed that it was true. I needed to sell my home and move to a place like this. In the meantime, I pictured sitting by a fireplace (on my right), and looking through sliding glass doors to a forest. I did it over and over again.

One year later, I was finally able to sell my home and move to a rural area in the mountains of Virginia. As in the vision, at the new home I could not see another house from my backyard. Also, I was able to find a job at a Garden Center a month or two after I moved to Virginia. An employee there reminded me of the man in the vision who was clipping the bushes. My new home had a fireplace and glass doors next to it.

SEEDS

Within our hopes and dreams the future lies waiting,
Like seeds sleeping till spring when they can awaken
And become what they were meant to be.

CHAPTER FIFTEEN

Seeing the "Web"

Another type of "vision" has also occurred. It is something that I am able to see almost anytime I want to see it. I just close my eyes almost all the way, but not quite. I have to be looking toward some kind of light, usually sunlight.

With my eyes almost closed I have seen a pale gray background, which seems to contain the shapes of veins or something like them. They are connected to each other with little ball-like circles. These make designs and have layers below them. Some are closer and more defined. This whole view seems to be moving and changing a little as I watch, like a living thing.

One time that I saw this, I saw a great many layers and it appeared to be almost like living lace. The top layer was usually very clear. It was delicate and the layers seemed to go on forever. There was no color accept gray, black and soft white. It moved gently. It was a delicate and beautiful dance. I was awed.

For many years I wondered what I was seeing. I doubted if I would ever find out the answer. Eventually, I moved to Florida and joined a Metaphysical Society. During one meeting, a member talked about an "energy grid" and her description sounded similar to what I had seen. I was amazed. I drew a quick picture and passed it to others in the room. They seemed to accept this as part of the energy grid. Perhaps it was true, but I may never really know for sure.

CHAPTER SIXTEEN

Clouds, Aura Work, Visualization in Traffic

I.
REIKI

Back when my children were in their teens, I took a short class from a Reiki Master that I knew personally. (She was the mother of one of my daughter's friends). At that time I brought in a few friends to share the cost of the class. We learned at that time, among other things, to move clouds. We put our hands up as though we could reach the clouds and pictured "swishing" them off to the sides. It actually worked. I was amazed.

Later, when my friend and I were going on an outing in the mountains, it started to rain. We had driven a long way and we didn't want to turn around and go home. So I suggested we try to move the clouds and stop the rain. I tried it while in the car and the rain stopped for a while. We also tried it when we arrived at our favorite mountain, Mt Major. We were able to open a small hole in the clouds so that we could have our lunch without interference. It never ceases to amaze me what we humans can do!

II.
RELAXATION TECHNIQUE

That day of the Reiki training I also learned how to smooth out someone's Aura. We practiced laying on the floor while our friends put their hands about three inches from the top of our head and brought those hands slowly and continuously down the body (still about three inches up) and then brought the hands under our feet. It was done over and over till the temperature of the reclining receiver felt even to the givers. The experience was wonderful for the recipient. After my turn, I did not want to get up. It was highly relaxing.

III.
VISUALIZATION

Back in the 1980's I bought some tapes that were helpful to me. One mentioned about visualization being very useful. In Chapter Four I mentioned how I used visualization to heal a dental issue. In this chapter I will address another use.

In one of the tapes that I acquired, the author said that he "arranged" to have a prime parking space wherever he went. He could picture it ahead of time - and it worked. He mentioned about working with traffic jams too. So, when sitting in traffic the next time, I decided to try to clear it. I visualized, the cars moving along way ahead of the line I was in at the time. I could "see" free flowing cars, and I moved my hands like I was brushing them along. If I could see it in my mind, it would seem to start things moving shortly afterward, albeit slowly. If I had trouble doing it, I usually discovered there was a good reason for the blocked traffic, for example an accident where the cars involved were not off the road yet. I still use that visualization as needed. I have done it enough times to catch on to the fact that it is no "coincidence".

IV.
JOB OFFER

Also in the 1980's, I was a temporary Administrative Assistant looking for a permanent position in a company where I worked. It came to my attention that they might be willing to hire me "for real". I had read or heard the tape about visualization recently. I decided to try it to see if I could get the job that way.

First I imagined an amount of money that I could accept and that they might be willing to offer me. Then I pictured entering my boss's office and being offered the job at that salary. I did that repeatedly and I prayed.

A few days later the opportunity I was expecting did occur. I was ushered into my boss' office and he told me that they would like to hire me. Would I accept the amount they offered? He told me what that was. It was the exact amount that I had pictured in my mind. I got the job.

BLESSINGS

The blessings of heaven are upon the wind -
Blowing through our lives
To land in the dry leaves of chance,
Awaiting our notice.

CHAPTER SEVENTEEN

Firewalk

Living in Florida has given me many opportunities that I found nowhere else. I have lived in five different states, plus I lived outside the country for two years. None of these other areas gave me the opportunities that I have had in Sun City Center, Florida. In the forum of the Metaphysical Society I have seen and heard amazing things and felt that I was with people like myself who have had experiences that were amazing and true. I could speak frankly there about what happened to me and get help with the situations that perplexed me.

One day I met a friend at the Metaphysical Society, who offered to bring me to a special Metaphysical church in Tampa. After a church experience there one day, I went with her to a presentation by a couple of men. According to their sign, they put on "Firewalks". These men explained the process to the audience. Several people signed up to participate. I wanted to sign up too, but I felt it was beyond my financial reach. When I spoke to these men, a deal was made so that I could participate. They found out that I was an artist and they asked if I would paint a picture of them doing a Firewalk. They would let me in for free if I could provide that. I provided the painting and was able to go to the event.

The day of the Firewalk, about thirty-five or forty people attended and formed a circle in the room. The two men who ran the group spoke to us and told us the rules. We were not to talk among ourselves and we were to pay strict attention, or the results could be dangerous. We could change our minds at any time if we chose.

One of the first things we did was to go outside and build the fire for the Firewalk. Then we went back in and participated in other activities, which led up to it. One of those was to break a board with our hand. We were prepared ahead on what it would take to accomplish this safely. Then we began. When we were ready, I saw almost everyone just walk up and break it. No one was hurt. I finally had the courage to try. Following the directions of the facilitators, I was able to do it the first time. It "blew me away"! The next activity was to walk on broken glass. This one seemed easy to me. I did it with no problem. We then were asked to place an arrow to our throat, and place the other end against a wall. We were told to stop holding it and push forward until it broke. (That was the hardest activity for me – but I eventually accomplished it.) Again no one was hurt. There was another activity with rebar, but I didn't participate in it.

Then we were ready for the Firewalk. The facilitators warned us also against trying this under any other circumstances. Do not do this at home… etc. After we took off our shoes and received some more very serious discussions and warnings, we went outside. We were told not to look down when we walked across the hot coals. We were not to walk across the hot coals of the fire unless we felt that we wanted to do it and felt ready. We had warnings again about the procedure. Then we started a chant and walked around the fire holding hands. There were two chants. The first one was Native American. The second one, I remembered well. It was "my body will do whatever it takes to protect me". This one was familiar. I had read it in a book that explained the mystery of the human body in that it "knows" things and does things automatically that are necessary for survival. I believed it. (I think that is probably the most important part of this.)

At about this point, the two men who facilitated the Firewalk began to walk across the coals. It was a walk of about 20 feet or more. They paid no attention to the fire and just spoke to each other as though they were walking across a parking lot.

Then a few of the participants decided to walk across the coals, and seemed to have no trouble at all (they had done it before and wanted to have another opportunity). We kept circling the fire over and over again and more people had the courage to do it. Each had no problem at all. I was amazed.

I did not feel up to it till near the end. Finally, I had a strong enough feeling of safety that I could do it too. I walked across it barefoot like all the others and I did not feel any heat. I was awed. A few minutes later I even did it again, this time I forgot I wasn't supposed to look down and began to feel the heat. I did not get burned, but just felt uncomfortable. How is it possible to do these things? I believe that faith played a part again.

FAITH

When we are filled with faith
And flowing over,
Joined by God -
All things are possible.

CHAPTER EIGHTEEN

HSP and Psychic Empathy

I.

HSP

For several years I traveled to New Hampshire from Florida and back by car to visit my family and friends, and go back to the natural areas that had impacted my life. During one such visit, I received a phone call from a dear friend in Florida who told me she had found a book that she wanted to share with me. There was a test inside the book to find out who was a "Highly Sensitive Person". My friend said she had qualified and she believed that I would also. We had a lot in common and I felt that she was very likely correct. The book's title is *The Highly Sensitive Person*, by Elaine Aron. I was intrigued. When the book arrived I took the test. I got 100%. The book discussed that in our society only about 10% of us are actually Highly Sensitive People. According to this book, I am at the top of that 10% group. That seems to say that I am in the top 1% out of 100 of the most sensitive people. The comments in this book suggest that our society, especially in the United States, is not set up for this group of people. We are not understood. However, we are responsible, conscientious creative people who are good employees.

I have known for a long time that I was sensitive. I have been highly sensitive to almost everything known. I feel extra sensitive to pain, cold, heat, spirituality, animals, other people's emotions, the spirit of nature, etc. I have often isolated myself from others because they have been unable to "see" this sensitivity. I often do not feel safe. I have spent a lot of time in nature, away from people for this reason.

II.
PSYCHIC EMPATHY

Also in Florida, I read another book, *Second Sight*, by Judith Orloff, and found a place in that book that discussed what it felt like to be a Physic Empath. The description gave me goose bumps. I suddenly realized that I was clearly one of these people. It suddenly made sense that I always seemed to feel everyone else's emotions with them. I don't seem to have a choice and even if it is inconvenient, I can't stop caring about what makes them happy. This explained a big part of my life, and my discomfort with being in big groups of people. I had learned early on to avoid that if I could. School was difficult for me for that reason. Even marriage became difficult as so few people I have met seem to be able to return that kind of caring.

Judith also discussed how to deal with all the "information" coming at those who have this ability. We have to "block" some of it. Judith discussed what it felt like to be on a bus and feel the emotions of someone behind you. She said it would be difficult to be in crowds. There is so much information and feelings coming through. It is confusing and uncomfortable.

I wrote a note to Judith Orwell, thanking her for her frank discussion of this topic. I told her that I thought she was a courageous person. She had impacted me greatly to let me know finally what was going on in my life.

ANGEL WORK

Often the work of angels, all unknown,
Secretly shows the way,
Till the light shines out -
Gloriously revealing the truth.

CHAPTER NINETEEN

Wood Fairy

When I lived in Florida, I lived in a community for the elderly, which boasted of having many kinds of clubs. A friend of mine suggested I go to the Metaphysical Club. I didn't even know what that meant at first. When she talked about it for a while, I decided I might try it. I waited a while, but eventually came to check it out. I found myself very comfortable there immediately and joined the club.

When I became part of the Metaphysical Club, many kinds of unusual ideas came to my attention. Also many new people joined the club. It grew weekly. One of the "new" people who showed up included a woman named "Mary". She had previously lived in Hawaii and had come to town to care for her ailing father. I could understand her challenges since I left my home and came to Florida to take care of my parents. I knew she was going to need a friend and I "volunteered". I invited her to join my little "Weekly Movie Group" of several friends who had been gathering at my home every week for a spiritual movie. She was happy to be one of them. That group eventually grew to ten people and included her ailing father.

One day Mary called me on the phone and told me that she had just returned from a doctor's visit to a medical intuitive. This doctor had come as a speaker to our Metaphysical meeting, so I was familiar with her. Mary explained that she told this woman she just met two new friends. She said I was one of them. The doctor told Mary that she wanted to "get in touch with Elizabeth's energy" - to see who I was. Once she had done so, she told Mary "Elizabeth is a very unusual and interesting person. She has the energy of a Wood Fairy".

When I heard this description, I was awed. Years before, I had decided that when I died I wanted to live in a forest and fly around in the trees and stay with nature, like a fairy. I could not think of better words to describe my soul. I thought "How could this woman know who I was and get it so perfect?"

WHEN I WAS YOUNG

When I was young
I loved the earth
And felt the joy
That it was worth.
I worshiped grass
And sun and trees
And felt God's love
In all of these.
My heart would pound
At the sight of the dawn.
I'd cry at the sight
Of the trees.
The love I bear
To all mankind
Is surely caused by these.

CHAPTER TWENTY

Dreams May Come True

I had been trying to sell my house in Florida since I bought it. However, it was not possible for several years. The housing market "hit the tank" about that time. I put it on the market several times and took it off again to wait for a better time. While I waited, I had some thinking and planning to do. I did it.

At this point, I also had a "reading" from a psychic person, Janet Reynolds, who had come to talk to our Metaphysical Group earlier. During my reading, she told me that dreams are messages. We should take them seriously. She said I would have what I want, but I have some work to do first. (There were other things she told me that will be discussed in anther chapter).

I had some dreams (in my sleep) and in a couple of them I saw houses. The first one I saw was an L- shaped old white farmhouse. The property around it did not have any trees to speak of and it did not really appeal to me for that reason. A few years later, I dreamed of a house and yard that was lovely. The home had a farmer's porch, which faced a small stream. I could see little yellow flowers in the grass and woods on the other side of the stream. I loved to just stare at it. The flowers moved gently in the breeze. One of my rather psychic friends checked with her pendulum to see if the house really existed. The result was that it did. I wasn't sure where.

Later, I thought that I might really sell my home and was looking on the Internet for homes in Virginia. I actually saw a home for sale that looked almost exactly like the dream I saw of the house on the edge of the stream in the woods. It existed near Roanoke Virginia. I felt like it was already mine. I imagined myself living there and sitting beside the stream. Somehow, I knew I could have it. When I finally arrived to see that house, it was obviously the house from my dream.

Later, I decided against this home due to other factors I discovered about the property. There was a questionable bridge over the stream to get to the house. The bridge was made of wood planks and some were missing. The house had a strong smell of tobacco and the person who had been living there was apparently a heavy drinker who hunted deer, all of which I found intolerable. I also found that it was very far from any type of stores. In back of the house was a very steep hill going upward. I felt sure it would not be a good thing in the rain. The water would wash toward the house. I felt a great loss in making the decision to walk away. I felt I had lost my dream house, but still it was important to me that it did exist.

Eventually I bought a house, which I believed was the "right one". I checked with another psychic, Reverend Ortrun Franklin, who was able to tell me which house was the one from the vision of "one year in the future". I mentioned it an earlier chapter. This house was also located in Virginia and now from the back yard I see only trees.

Later, after I moved in to my new home, I found out that there was another individual who helped me to accomplish this move, one who is mentioned in a later chapter.

Mysteries abound upon our dear Earth
In the secret recesses of her soul . . .
And when we open her gifts
We feel her magic.

CHAPTER TWENTY-ONE

Lamp Lighting

In the Meditation Group I attended, there was a woman who I was told had lost her husband. I spoke with her later. From discussions with her, I heard that she felt her husband did not want to leave her. He decided to stay with her in his new state. As the story goes, he lights a light in her bedroom whenever she is there. She sometimes turns it off and he turns it right back on. Or she will turn it off, to go somewhere, and when she gets home he turns it on again. It happens every single day and is still happening as I write. I have thought of this lady often.

A year or two went by, and one day I saw a light go on, then off, in my living room. I remembered that lady and I felt curious. I decided to find out what was happening. I wondered if it was a bad wire. But also, I have felt for a long time that my grandfather was with me. Since we were very close when he was alive, I felt he was watching over me, as in one of the previous chapters. I wanted to know now if he was turning the light on. I spoke to the "air" (to him) asking if he was doing it, and if so, would he do it again. The light went on, then off again.

In January 2010 I had another session with Janet Reynolds. She told me that my father was there and wanted me to "keep an eye" on my brother. I decided to honor his wishes and got in contact with my brother. We agreed to meet and take a walk together on that Friday. We met and had a nice conversation and walked with the dog. He held the leash.

Soon after I arrived home, the lamp in my living room went on again by itself. Then it went off. No other lights did that. It also reminded me about my grandfather. I asked again if it was he, and if so, would he light the lamp again. The light went on. It never turned on by itself again. I "knew" that my grandfather was glad when I got in touch with my brother.

Unknown dreams
Soft spoken,
Gentle token,
Love to come,
All unknown,
Begotten of peace.

CHAPTER TWENTY-TWO

Eyes

When my first granddaughter was born, her mother (my daughter) remembered she had seen a large group of Monarch butterflies around the time my granddaughter was conceived. She thought it was some kind of sign and that they were associated with her first child. She taught her daughter about butterflies and asked me to paint a mural with monarchs on my granddaughter's bedroom wall, which I did.

Several years later I bought a digital camera. Since then, I have taken literally thousands of pictures. Due to my granddaughter's interest in butterflies and my interest in photography, I took a "plethora" of photos of butterflies. One day I made the momentous decision to identify them. This led me to an almost overpowering wish to get photographs of all the types of butterflies in Florida. I bought a very helpful book written by a butterfly expert at the University of Florida. It fueled my continued interest.

One day, my friend Jeanette called and told me that a lady reporter in our area wanted to write an article about someone who knew about butterflies. Jeanette thought I should give her a call. I had been planting for the butterflies, and many had grown up in the garden in front of my house. I had several bushes filled with butterflies in my backyard and I often went on "adventures" to find butterflies and photograph them in gardens and wild places. I found two butterfly exhibits with live butterflies and was able to walk around within an enclosed area with hundreds of butterflies. I was always busy trying to find any butterflies that I had not photographed yet. It seemed to me I might be just the lady for whom this woman was looking.

I called the reporter and she decided to come out and interview me. Later, one of my butterfly photos showed up on the cover of the magazine accompanying the Tampa Tribute. They had a two-page article about my hobby including a picture of me with my fennel plant where all "my" Black Swallowtails had been 'born". I began to be called the "Butterfly Lady".

Many people have seen me deep in the weeds in a frozen position or running after butterflies with my camera. I go everywhere that the butterflies appear. It has led me to many wild places. One day it led me to an area next to a savings bank where there were trees on a gently rolling piece of land next to the main street through our town. I had seen some butterflies from a distance and I wanted to find them. They were elusive and I was stalking them with camera in my face. I could hardly see where I was going.

I thought I spied a new one, but had difficulty seeing it because I saw so many devas in the way (to be discussed in chapter 27), when suddenly two very clear, brown eyes slid slowly into view from the right. The eyes were *round*. They were not human eyes and there was no body or head to go with them! More than that, they were eyes that showed emotion. They looked directly into mine. The eyes seemed to say with some anger "And what do you think you are doing here!" or "be careful where you are stepping!" and then they slid back again to the right. They were very close and very clear. I wish I had clicked the photo! This experience had frightened me so much that I did not realize at the time that I could have taken a picture of those eyes. However, I knew for sure that I had seen something highly unusual! All kinds of wild thoughts crowded my brain. Was this a creature from outer space? Was it a bad spirit? What could it be? I felt very strongly that I *had* to find out what, or who, that was! Who could I ask? Who in the world would know? Of course! I knew it could be none other than Carl Franklin.

About a year later, Carl Franklin, was visiting our Metaphysical Group. I had a moment when I could walk up and ask a question after his speech. I told him about the experience. He and his wife Ortrun, tried to guess the identity of the being with the mysterious eyes. Carl's wife finally came up with the idea that they should check to see if it was a Leprechaun. I stood there in shock. They had to be kidding! I didn't believe in Leprechauns!

Carl Franklin used his pendulum to ask whether it was actually a Leprechaun. The answer was yes! You can imagine how I felt? But now that I have had a while to adjust, I believe in them now! There is more to this story and it will continue in other chapters.

Friends can hold the secrets of the universe.
They are the gifts of God,
Given to those who are ready.

CHAPTER TWENTY-THREE

Mom

I have mentioned coming to live in Florida before this, but here is more information about it. This leads to another adventure.

In 2002, I came to Florida. My parents could not live alone any longer as reported by my sister. She had found my mother unconscious on the floor. She had been helping them for some time and was apparently desperate for my help. She called me and begged me to come. My job was ending anyway so I left my home in New Hampshire and I stayed with them in their home for about nine months before my mother passed away. Then, after a little more than a year my father passed away too. My two siblings and I buried the ashes of our parents, first my mother and then my father, in a wild area a couple of miles from their home. That was what they wanted.

One day my brother and I went to visit the gravesite of my mother. When we arrived, my brother told me he would wait for me to go and "do my thing" at the grave and he would be second. So I walked over into the wooded area where her ashes were buried. I stood there a couple of minutes and talked to her as people do in the movies. I told her that I knew that she was happy now that she didn't have that body any longer. She had no more pain or worries. "I had tried to tell you it would be great, and now you must know how wonderful it is on the other side", I said. I was happy for her.

Shortly after I said that, I *saw* something like a mist or smoke coming out of the ground where she was buried and coalescing into the general shape of a human. I immediately "knew" it was my mother. I "saw" her move/fly over to me and knew somehow that she put her arm around me. Before she died I had told her I needed more hugs from my parents. Maybe she finally responded to my request!

Later people started calling me Catherine, which was my mother's name. It seemed odd. First, Carl's wife, Ortrun, called me Catherine and I told her that my name was Elizabeth. She asked me if I knew anyone by that name. I said it was my mother's name and she had passed away. At that I was told that my mother must be was with me. Then others called me Catherine also.

I am often awed by the way God has created this world and the things that are made possible. That is why I wrote:

GODS PRESENCE

Sometimes in the twilight
When I'm sitting quietly,
I remember times of challenge,
When God was there for me.
Sometimes He has spoken
In words I could not hear,
And sometimes in the forest
His message seemed so clear.

The voice of God's in silence,
In the wind among the trees,
In songs of thrush and sparrow,
In things He makes like these.
God's with me in the faith I hold
So closely to my breast,
He gives my soul what's needed –
A sense of peace and rest.

CHAPTER TWENTY-FOUR

Messages for Me

I.
GRANDPA

When I decided to have another reading from someone new at our little metaphysical group, Tilley Hagen. During our time together, she told me that my mother was in the room with me. It was very definite that my grandfather was there also. He came forward out of the group of five or six spirits to let me to know that he was proud of me, and that, like him, I would "do whatever it took". I was grateful for the support. It also underscored the fact that I already felt his presence and probably heard his voice earlier calling my name. But he was also right.

II.
MOM

The first time that Janet Reynolds came to our little Metaphysical Group and gave messages from the "other side", she came up to me after the meeting and told me my mother wanted to give me some messages. I was awed. I hadn't even asked Janet any questions. She said that my mother wanted me to know, that I was "taking things too seriously" and "doing too much". It sounded just like her. She keeps showing up.

III.
REIKI SESSION

Living in Florida was tough for me financially and I often wondered about renting a room in my home to help me with the bills. One day I received a newsletter from a church I had visited for a while. It was a surprise that they sent me one since I had left that church a long while before that.

I decided I would look through the publication quickly and throw it out. Normally I would just have thrown it away immediately, but for some "unknown" reason I didn't. On the back page was a request to find someone who would rent a room in their house. Cautiously, I called to find out more about this person and the circumstances. I immediately heard "So you are the Angel". I was perplexed but curious why the woman would say that.

During the rest of the conversation I heard that the potential renter was a therapist and a metaphysically oriented individual. I decided we would have some things in common and I wanted to speak directly with her about the possibility of renting my extra room. The woman's name was Teri. In my conversation with her, I found out that she had gone to a psychic and was told there would be one "Angel" who would take her in, and that person would welcome her with open arms. This person would be a "survivor" and an artist. I met those qualifications. It felt like fate, or God's intervention in our lives. There were no other responses to her advertisement.

Teri lived with me for several months during the time she was looking for a house. She said she would give me a Reiki session sometime. When she finally got around to it, she amazed me. She did much more than that. She could see my grandfather and my mother among others standing nearby. She also gave me another session a year or two afterwards. This time she told me that my mother stood near my head and made a point of saying that she was "here too!"

Also, in a Reiki session with my friend Teri, I was told that there was an Angel there who wanted me to know that I could call on it anytime. (They are not male or female.) This was my "Official Angel" it said. Teri said it had beautiful wings and a white flowing robe, as many paintings of Angels show. That was why it called itself my "Official Angel". Now, I get help when I ask. (Having a lot of "senior moments", I ask pretty often.)

This Angel helps me to find things I have misplaced. Sometimes I ask for safety. It seems to be working. I always find the things I am looking for and I have been safe in my home. There are things that people are not supposed to ask and I avoid them, such as winning the lottery... (I goofed once, before I found this Angel, and asked for that.) I won ten dollars though. I was also "feeling" the numbers on that occasion to see if they "felt" like the right ones. Then I quit trying.

It is nice to know that God has these amazing helpers. I thank God for them. It seems sometimes that humans can be working for God also, and I am grateful. Teri is one. Many more are listed in the "Acknowledgements" page. They all played "Angel" for me.

CHAPTER TWENTY-FIVE

Marge, Jack and Catherine

I.
MARGE

I mentioned earlier about my Aunt Marge. She was a my favorite aunt, and my children's as well. When we found that she had bone cancer, it was devastating. We all were walking around in a miserable fog. We watched her fight it for five years and finally loose. My sister, sister-in-law and my eldest daughter, were in her home helping as much as they could during the last month of her life. I visited her in the hospital every day but I was not able to be present after she went back home. I was only able to come back on the day she died. All we women were in my aunt's room for some time during that day. Eventually, I had walked into another room briefly. A minute later my sister called from the other room to say that our aunt was passing. I ran back in but was too late. Fortunately, I had said good-by earlier.

We all waited for the funeral parlor to send someone to pick her up. While I waited, it occurred to me that I had read stories of people who passed away and came back to tell about it. They said that they found themselves looking down from above at their bodies. They could see other people around them from that perspective for a while.

I decided to "feel my way" around the room with my eyes and my heart. I especially checked out the ceiling. I thought that I had found her near the edge of the ceiling where it met the wall nearest to her room. I was just outside the door from the room. I had never tried to do that before, but to this day, I suspect she was really there looking at me. I looked up at her and smiled and said "hi" and "I love you". I figured it was worth a try.

II.
JACK

My sister got divorced after 25 years of marriage. She went to Florida at that point to stay for a while with my parents. She found a man there with whom she fell in love. His name was Jack. I was delighted. It seemed as though she was very happy. Jack lived with his blind mother. He took care of his mother until she died. Then he asked my sister to live with him and she accepted. He wanted to marry her, but she did not believe in marriage any longer. He had to be happy with what he could get. Unfortunately, he was a very sick man. He died about a year later.

When I heard that he had died in his sleep next to her one night, I felt sad for my sister. I just knew somehow that she would need me. I took a plane down from New Hampshire and stayed for about a week.

During the beginning of my stay I remember walking into my sister's bedroom, the one she had shared with him, and I had a strong sense that Jack was sitting on the bed smiling and watching us. In a way I could "see" him. I remember telling my sister that he was there. I was sure this time!

III.
CATHERINE

Just a note: After having these other experiences, it was even easier to believe that my mother was with me when I "saw" her come out of her grave. (Mentioned previously)

CHAPTER TWENTY-SIX

Healing With Prayer

I.
MOTHER

My mother had Chronic Leukemia for about 20 years. The doctors "watched" her during that time and did tests and procedures on her, some of which were extremely painful. Being a nurse, she understood and did not complain. For many years, she lived in Florida and I lived in New Hampshire so we did not communicate as easily as if I lived nearby. Sometimes I did not find out what she was enduring until later. I remember writing her a loving poem to let her know I was thinking of her with great affection.

One day I was told that she was in the hospital with an infection behind her eye that had not responded to any of the normal treatments. She was in ICU. Her life could end at any moment. I felt that all I could do was pray. I was told that the doctors had done all they could.

In church, where I sang in the choir, there was a part of the service where they asked if anyone needed prayers. I held up my hand and discussed the situation regarding my mother. The whole congregation prayed for her. I also prayed again before and after the service.

The next day I received a phone call discussing the state of my mother's health. It seems that in the "eleventh hour" the doctors decided to try an experimental medication on her, not knowing if it would actually work. It was the only medication left to try. It *did* work. She was out of trouble.

I could breathe again . . . at least for a while. I believe our prayers helped.

II.
GRANDDAUGHTER

One day my youngest daughter called me to say that my little granddaughter was diagnosed with a severe form of scoliosis. The doctor was very concerned. This child was about five years old and would very likely have to wear a body brace almost continuously the rest of her life, and experience a great deal of trouble and discomfort. It looked very bad for her future. The whole family was frightened. There did not appear to be much hope for her healing.

When I got off the phone with my daughter, I thought about the situation and came up with an idea that I thought might work. At least I hoped that it would heal her without all the dismal discomforts that the medical community might cause her to endure.

I asked a group of my dearest friends to pray for my granddaughter. We prayed together that night. There were about six of us. I also called my daughter and told her of my plan and mentioning our prayers. Additionally, I told her that she might be able to heal her child on her own as well. I told her to ask her child to lie face down on her bed, then she was to sit down next to her child and slowly put her hands on her neck and move them slowly down her spine, but she must also feel the love for her dear daughter and picture that love going into the affected areas in her spine as she proceeded. My daughter was to use all the love she had in her heart and place it in her hands picturing it moving into those areas. She said she would do it.

When my granddaughter went to her doctor on the next visit, the doctor *could not find any sign of the scoliosis.* He was amazed. He could not understand it. Her next appointment was put off for a year. So far the problem has not returned. Either one, or both of these processes could have made this "miracle" a reality. You decide.

III.
BABY

In one of the places where I worked, I heard about a one week old child who had been born with a severe heart problem. The doctors believed the baby would need a heart transplant as soon as possible in order to survive. They needed a heart. One of the men that worked with me was related to the child. He said that he was asking for prayers for this little one. Those who wanted to pray for the child did so. We were told also that certain churches were sharing this information with their parishioners and they were praying too. It seemed that a great number of people were coming together to help this baby fight for his life. We all hoped they could find a heart for this child. There was an article in the local paper to that effect.

Within a few weeks we heard that a donor had been found for the child and the transplant was successful. Children all need hope, even those that cannot speak. I believe God answered those prayers

PRAY FOR ME
(Letter from a child)

Pray for me
In the secret corners of your heart
Where love resides,
And God will bless your prayers.

I cannot speak
To tell you what you need to know -
That I love you so,
But I will never forget.

Pray for me
And God will hear
And bless your life
Forever.

CHAPTER TWENTY-SEVEN

Orb and Deva Photography

I.
READING

As mentioned earlier, Carl Franklin, is a metaphysical researcher, psychologist, and minister, who I met for the first time in Florida at the Metaphysical Society. He spoke to our group and offered to give a "reading" to any who would like one. For the first time in my life I decided to try it. I paid what I thought was a reasonable price and he gave me a "reading" related to why I was here and what Angels, Masters, etc. may be "over-lighting me" etc.

During that session, which he taped, I found out some fascinating things, which I won't go into in this context, but this is where I was told that I would be able to see "devas". I could see him asking in his special way if I would be able to see them, and watched the answers "arrive". A "yes" was more than obvious! He explained what they were, and I found out these devas were really anxious for me to make contact. That was a sure thing! He encouraged me strongly to talk to them. There was a part of me at the time that wondered if all this was a bit crazy. It was "out there", but my curiosity got to me.

I went home that day, walked into my Lanai in Florida, and sat down next to my group of Christmas cactuses. I looked at them carefully and felt silly, but determined. (I swore I would never tell anyone about this!)

I proceeded to ask if the Devas would please appear to me. I said I was told that they might *want* to do that. I also said that it would be a very big honor for me.

It was within about 15 seconds that I started to see little circular snowflake-like beings made of light. I was amazed. There were about four or five of them. A few didn't seem to want to stay for long and disappeared. They might have been about a half an inch or less in diameter. (I couldn't measure them!) One or two of them seemed to suddenly loose the top half, then they would either disappear or come back to their original and complete shape. These devas had what I like to call an "eye" in them that was off center.

I stared at the "devas" for several minutes afraid to move, and then it occurred to me that I could ask the other plant in the room if it would also share with me it's deva. I wondered if they would be larger due to the fact that it was a much larger plant. To my amazement and delight, it took only a moment before I saw its deva. It was after I went through the same request process. They were indeed larger, and they appeared round and made of light too. A few of the small ones showed up in my living room that night.

II.
INTRODUCTION TO DEVAS

Recently, I received an e-mail message from my friend Carl Franklin and his wife Ortrun, which included this description regarding (not just plant) Devas:

> **Deva Kingdom:** *Physical Elementals who aid Angelic Realms and Councils of Elohim in formulating and maintaining many elements which make up Physical Creation.*

In the words of Machaelle Small Wright, who wrote a book called *Behaving as if the God in All Life Mattered,* devas are described this way:

DEVA (pronounced: day´-vah) is the Sanskrit word for "body of light." I found the devic level to be a level of consciousness very high in vibration. It's as if someone were to hit a bunch of tuning forks and we could distinguish the vibratory difference between them rather than the sound difference. I found the devic vibration to feel extremely high and light. It did not even resemble anything I had experienced in meditation previously. Its essence was clearly different. The word "architect" has been used by others when describing what devas do—and I, also, find this to be the most appropriate word. For example, it is the devic level that designs the blueprint and draws together all the various energies that make up the complex "package" for the carrot. The Carrot Deva "pulls together" the various energies that determine the size, color, texture, taste, growing season, nutritional needs, shape, flower and seed process of the carrot. In essence, the Carrot Deva is responsible for the carrot's entire physical package. It maintains the vision (the complete reality) of the carrot in perfection and holds that collection of energies together in their unique pattern as it passes from one vibratory level to another on its route to becoming physical to the five senses. Everything about the carrot on a practical level, as well as on the more expanded, universal level, is known by the Carrot Deva.*

In my own words, I would like to add: As dogs can hear sounds that are a higher vibration than humans can hear, these beings are at a higher vibration of energy, regarding sight, among other things. Humans have not been able to see them. As far as I am aware at this point, I was the first to see them and then to photograph them. I have also shown others how to see them. I believe that they are conscious and are coming to

---

a point where they would like to be recognized. According to Carl Franklin, the elementals (which include devas), want me to be their representative. When I heard that, I was awed. I also heard later that I was supposed to publish something. At first I did not know what to publish. Now I know. You are reading it.

In Machaelle's book *Behaving As If The God In All Life Mattered,* she informs us that plant devas started communicating with her about how to create and care for her garden. After some confusion, she discovered who they were. That communication continues on today as far as I know. Machaelle wrote a very much in-depth description regarding devas and the information she received. If you are curious enough to read her book, you may be delighted and intrigued by the information she shares.

Again, from my observation, plant devas are often about 1/8 inch, possibly larger, in diameter. They are beautiful, fragile and more delicate than a snowflake. At first I thought they were round, but in the photos they seem to have five or six sides. Plant devas differ in color, design and size depending on the type of plant they represent. Please see the front and back covers for color photos.

III.
AWAY WE GO

Plant devas showed up often after that. I noticed that they appeared on my glasses. They showed up mostly when I was outdoors. I went to parks and found them and when I was just walking around in the neighborhood. I saw them at a shopping mall once with my friend Mary. I took off my glasses and handed them to her. She saw them for the first time.

I called another friend, Jeanette, one day and asked her if she would like to see devas. She was intrigued. We agreed to make the attempt at a park about a half an hour away. We met there and walked into the park, stopping to face the wooded area near us. I then addressed the local deva population with the something like following words: "Hello. If there are devas out there, I love you. I respect you and what you do. I have been honored to know about you and have seen your kind many times. I would like to know if you would be willing to show yourselves to my friend who is a loving and trustworthy person. Like me she would also be very honored if you would show yourselves to her." Then Jeanette addressed them herself lovingly. In a while I asked her if she saw anything. She said "yes". Two of them had appeared. She was not wearing glasses at the time, which I thought was an important distinction. Later I saw a few that were not on my glasses either.

I feel like plant devas are my friends. I am grateful when they sit on my glasses, many times on the edges and sometimes on the "glass". They keep me company. Some of them are very colorful. Some seem to have eyes. Interestingly, they seem to be absent when I am driving the car, I presume because they would not want to cause an accident, but perhaps there is another reason. They also have appeared on the lens of my camera when I took photos, which most often were of butterflies. Once I saw so many devas that I could hardly see what I was trying to photograph. Then I saw "the eyes" (described in another chapter).

Eventually I was able to draw pictures of plant devas. I used those pictures when I gave a report about them at the Metaphysics group in my community in Florida. I included all the information that I had picked up in my adventures with these usually invisible, amazing and beautiful life forms.

Still, I wished that I could take photographs of them. I was unsure that they would be willing to cooperate in that regard. They seemed so wary of people. However, my wish was finally granted while I was visiting Winnikinni Park, in Haverhill, MA. While there, the idea dawned on me that I might get their permission to photograph them. I found some devas on my glasses and then asked if they would *please* let me take their pictures. I could hardly breathe when I put the glasses down and grabbed the camera. I looked through the lens and they were *still there*. I zoomed in to get the shot and clicked. When I looked at what I had caught, I was awed. They *did* show up. I thanked them and felt blessed. Now I can share them with you. See the first photo on the left. Photo 1.

Then I went back to Mt. Major in New Hampshire and found I could also take photos of Devas I found there. See the photos of Devas at Mount Major near Alton Bay.

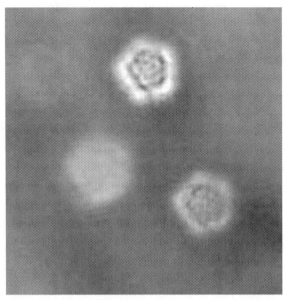

Photo 1, Devas at Winnikinni Park, Haverhill, MA

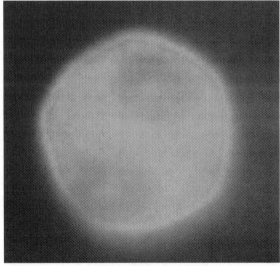

Photo 2, Devas at Mt. Major (one on my glasses)

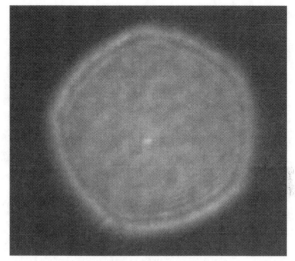

Photo 3, "Blue Deva"

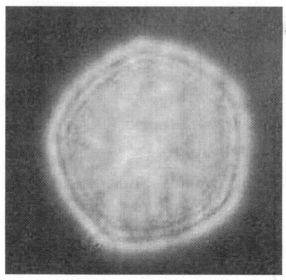

Photo 4, "Striped Deva"

Photo 5, Close-up of Devas at Mt. Major in NH – A

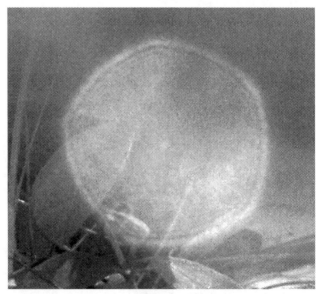

Photo 6, Close-up of Deva at Mt. Major in NH - B

IV.
SPIRIT ORBS

I call this next type "Spirit Orbs" because my friend Jeanette saw three faces inside the first one I shared with her. (I saw two when I looked back at it.) They are almost always pink with the outer area of it transparent. One photo I took at Gettysburg was different. It was solid pink.

This adventure began one day when I was taking a photo of my front walkway, where I had just planted some new flowers. I looked at my photos later, and was astounded to see a large pink orb that I could almost see through. It was at least a foot or more across and part of it was *behind* the small wall next to the garden. That means to me that it was *not* a smudge on my camera lens. This was when I showed it to a friend, who later said she saw three people in the orb. Upon further study of the photo, I found two. The face of a lady is the easier one to see. Her face is in the middle of the orb. The eyes are not quite human. The orb was at least one foot in diameter. The other face in the orb looked like a strange male being. I suspect they are Nature Spirits (if they are not our imagination). They may be in the Fairy realm. I hoped they would show up for me. This was the first in a series of photos with a pink orb showing up only *after* I took the picture. So far I have found that they are invisible otherwise.

Next, I took a photo on a trail near the garden in Sun City Center, which the locals call "Tillers and Toilers". When I arrived home and saw the photo, I was amazed to find another of these pink orbs. This one seemed quite large also. It was not all the way in the picture either. It seemed to have an outside area that was more transparent than the center, but this time there was a design inside the outer edge, unlike the first one I caught in a photo. See Photo 9.

I went on vacation to New Hampshire that year after discovering these wonderful natural beings. During my trip I took pictures at Skyline

Drive in Virginia and caught another one near the edge of the photo of the mountain panorama. (This photo is on the cover of the book.)

I also went to Gettysburg Pennsylvania on my way back and forth from New Hampshire and took photos there. A plain pink orb showed up in that picture afterward also. There did not appear to be a transparent edge on this one. See photo 11.

Some time later I found an old photo of the Tillers and Toilers garden and saw another pink orb. See photo 10.

Photo 7. Spirit Orb in Florida /Note wall on left

Photo 8. Spirit Orb in Florida Close-Up

Photo 9, Spirit Orb Near Common Garden

Photo 10, Spirit Orb at Sun City Center, FL in the
common garden (Tillers and Toilers)

Photo 11. Spirit Orb at Gettysburg, PA

V.
THIRD TYPE OF ORB

In this section I will be discussing another type of orb, which seems to be consistently similar wherever they appear. See the next photos. They are not pink or tiny. They seem to be pale, multi-colored and soft and several inches in diameter.

In May of 2011, I decided to build a bridge over the stream in my backyard. When I was finally able to walk across it, I called my friend in Florida and told her about it. I told her also of that beautiful area. It seemed to be magical and even a holy place. She asked me to take photos and send them.

I brought my camera down to the stream the next day, which was dark and rainy. I had to use a flash for the photos. When I got around to putting the photos onto my computer, I noticed a light in the photo that did not seem to make sense. I remember saying to myself "what is that doing there?" There are no houses there or any kind of manmade structures. Only God walks there. I was very surprised. I believe it is another form of nature being in another dimension, (Photo 13). It is difficult to identify what they represent. They have been just called orbs by many other people. This orb was different from the "spirit orbs" or "devas" in previous photos. Now I have photographed two alike. One was in another person's yard, (Photo 12). Unless it followed me, they look very similar.

Photo 12, Local Virginia Orb
Photo taken in a friend's yard

See below for the other photo of the same type orb seen in my yard back by my bridge (in the middle of the woods over a stream). Again, there are no homes and the land goes down to a V shape where the stream crosses my property.

Photo 13. "Orb" in my yard

The orbs above also look very much like the cover photo on a DVD I bought - *Orbs - The Veil is Lifting.* Many people believe that nature is changing and so are we. Perhaps this is only the beginning of a great adventure of discovery. You may see one in a photo soon if you have one of these older digital cameras. It has been suggested, in this documentary DVD "Orbs", that these beings are presently in a different/ higher dimension that only a few digital cameras are able to "see" at this point. My camera was bought in 2004 so apparently it was one of the old ones.

VI.
FOURTH TYPE OF ORB

The next type of orb is much larger than the others. They appear to be about two feet across. Of course I did not see them at all when looking through the viewfinder to take the photo. Later, the contrast was intensified on my computer to show the orbs better in the final picture. As you can see many of the orbs near the floor overlap in the photo and some of them are more obvious than others.

The history of this photo (plate 14) was the following: In July 2011, a man (and his wife) put in the walls and ceiling of my garage. I planned to give them a picture to show others his good work. I took the photo of him in my garage completely unsuspecting that these orbs would show up afterward. I have wondered why they came. There was however joy on all our parts, plus the results of creativity, which may have drawn these amazing beings (in my humble opinion).

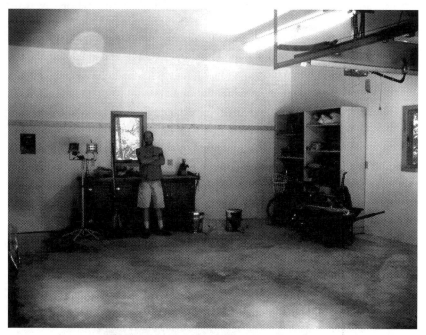

Photo 14, Orbs in My Garage, July 2011

In the documentary DVD, *Orbs - The Veil is Lifting*, you may find some more clues to the questions about these amazing beings. It includes the authors of *The Orb Project*. On the front of the DVD it suggests that this may be just the beginning of our discoveries in this matter. The orbs in this video are many sizes. "Experts" discuss their experiences. One man on the video tried a test to see what would happen if he took a photo when his son tried to bring his consciousness outside his head on command. (I have heard of such a thing before in a book, but have not been able to do it yet.) He took the picture and explained that he found an orb showed up next to his son's head. Perhaps one could extrapolate and say that these orbs are the consciousness of various beings that may even be human. Maybe we will find out soon.

VII.
FIFTH TYPE OF ORB

The following photos show some type of orbs. (I am still wondering if these show up due to a camera glitch.) However, they show up only when I take photos of flowers, butterflies or hummingbirds and it is usually getting late in the day. They look tiny in comparison to most of the other types. Maybe they are devas? I have seen these kinds of "orbs" sometimes if I do not focus my eyes.

Photo 15, Orbs in my garden July 2011

Photo 16. Hummingbird Feeder with Orbs

CHAPTER TWENTY-EIGHT

The Spirit of the Elephant

In February of 2011, I went on a vacation to Florida from my Virginia home. My aim was to go to the "Coptic Conference" which has been a once a year event. I was planning to visit my brother and some old friends. I brought my traveling companion, Liz, with me. My friend Mary asked us to come for dinner and wanted some independent quality time. Only Liz and I were invited. Liz and Mary were talking for a while alone. My eyes and my mind wandered and a new "adventure" began.

I looked across the room and saw two beautiful wooden carved elephants next to each other. I was drawn to them. I walked over and sat on a chair next to them. I reached out and started to stroke them gently. I began to remember all the amazing information I had heard about elephants. They were supposed to be one of the three animals on earth that had the highest and most beautiful love energy. I also remembered how horribly humans had treated them over the centuries. I felt a great connection to them. I could relate to them. I touched them even more lovingly and gently and eventually began to cry. Tears rolled down my cheeks for what they had endured. I could see it all in my mind's eye, the abuse and torture of these gentle beasts. Then I decided to tell "the elephants" how I felt. I called out to the "top elephant" the Deva / "Spirit of the Elephants". I "sent" out the love and compassion with all of my heart as the tears continued down my cheeks.

Shortly after I "sent" my message, I saw clearly to my great surprise, the eye of an elephant looking at me. You could have "knocked me over with a feather" as they say! All around the eye was the wrinkled skin I knew so well. I could only see that part of him. He looked right at me, into my soul, with much kindness and love. I could tell he was glad that I cared. He stayed with me for what felt like a long time. I finally had to get up and I went into the other room looking for Kleenex to wipe my tears. He followed me and suddenly I saw the whole of him.

At that point it occurred to me that it would be fun to go for a ride on his back. He seemed to suggest that I do just that. I could *feel* his feelings. I loved the idea and so did he. I proceeded to put my leg up on his back and perched myself up there. Immediately I lay down forwards and put my arms around his neck with my head down on his leathery skin. I gave him a great loving and happy hug. I felt safe and loved back. I stayed that way for a minute or so, then sat up and joyfully put my arms out straight to each side as we took off walking through the forest which had suddenly appeared. It was amazing and totally delightful walking through his leafy domain in that way. I was grateful to be somehow transported to his kingdom.

Eventually I realized I had to get back to my friends. I didn't want to leave my newfound loving, companion, but I knew that I would have to go back to the "real world". I felt that I had been with him in a different type of existence. It was a little like being in the "Twilight Zone" (if you are old enough to remember that show).

When we said good-bye, I was sad. I don't know if I will get another chance to be with that wonderful being, but I hope so. I feel like we are now friends forever.

Friends are precious gifts to be unwrapped during the
adventures of our lives . . . and treasured forever.

CHAPTER TWENTY-NINE

Send Them to the Light

I.
BACKGROUND

When I was a teenager, I stayed with my Aunt Marge and family for the summer. During that time my cousin Tom would share with me some of what he considered to be the best books he had read. His walls were covered with bookshelves and all the books located there were those he had read. One of those books was *Life After Life* by Raymond A. Moody. In this book the author shared a lot of research with those who had died and then came back to life. There were a surprising number of people who had that experience. In this book, most of those who went through this had experienced a dark tunnel with a light at the end of it. They would choose to walk towards that light. That light would bring them to a "heavenly place". I found it very interesting. I did not know that I would ever meet anyone who had the experience of dying and coming back, but I did, twice as an adult. Then, I also read a book by a lady who died and was dead for four hours before she "came back". She saw this "light" and found Jesus at the end of the tunnel. The title of the book is *Embraced by the Light*, by Betty Eadie.

From experience with my mother, reading a number of books, and talking to two people who died and returned, I have found that it is very important to walk to the light, and in a timely fashion, when you "pass on". If you don't, you "get stuck". You are not going where you are supposed to go. It is not good for you. Some people just hang around as "ghosts" or "spirits" after they "pass on", either because they don't believe in God, they want to solve a problem of some kind, or they don't know how it works. I have run into a couple of spirits who just didn't go because they didn't know how things work. Some did not seem to want to leave their loved ones.

II.
THE LEPRECHAUN

The first example concerns the Leprechaun that I mentioned in another chapter. I said I would get back to him again. This is that time.

When I found out that I had seen an actual Leprechaun, I was shocked. Then I was intrigued. The information simmered in my mind for a while, and finally I decided I wanted to see if he was still at the same location and try to talk to him. I wanted to meet him. I thought we had some things in common. I was partly Irish (Farrel is an Irish name after all) and I loved nature. I also loved to sing and dance and knew the Irish Jig. So I rode my bicycle over to where I had seen him and sang an Irish song. I picked up all the trash in the area (partly because I heard they liked conservation minded people). I tried to let him know that we could be friends. I actually invited him to my home.

I think it was a day or two after that, when I was about to get out of my car in the garage. It felt as though my left earring was pulled off. It seemed to fall down by the door. I couldn't find it. I thought I must have caused it. I just dismissed the event. The next day I was in the garage preparing to exit the car again. This time my right earring was actually pulled off. I *knew* it this time. I hadn't moved in any way to cause it. At this point I knew with whom I was dealing. I said to my invisible "friend" that I could appreciate his sense of humor, but I *did* want my earring back. I was able to find that earring on the floor. I invited him in. It was the week of St. Patrick's Day (appropriately). I decided to celebrate it that year by getting decorations and showing him an Irish movie. I wanted to make him feel at home. I used my pendulum to find out if he would like to watch the movie. The answer was yes. (I asked him directly and expect that he was the one that really moved the pendulum.) We had a nice day.

After a while I wondered why my new friend was in Sun City Center, Florida. It seemed odd. I wondered if he would rather go back to Ireland. I told him that if I were he, I would want to go home. I asked him through the Pendulum if he wanted to go home. The answer was yes. I decided I would help him. I got on the computer to find out about plane flights etc. I planned to drive him to the airport. I figured he could get on without needing a ticket. Nobody would see him. I was in uncharted territory here. It felt weird! Fortunately, I was getting used to weird!

Later I talked to my friend Mary (who taught me how to use a pendulum incidentally), and she said that he didn't need my help to go anywhere. I was perplexed and finally called Carl Franklin. Carl checked with his dowsing rods, or a pendulum, and told me that the Leprechaun had died and could not find his way to get to the "light". He was going to help send him there. He told me to tell "my Leprechaun friend" what he was telling me over the phone. So I gave my new "friend" the information. Carl called in the "Angels of Transition", and the deceased members of his family which would come and "get" him. Carl told me he watched as the Leprechaun's family came to pick him up. He told me that my friend danced the Irish Jig because he was so happy to see his family. I felt delighted to be a part of his joy. It took me a while to get used to all this. It doesn't happen every day!

Next, Carl told me that the Leprechaun might return sometime and do something nice for me, and it seems that he *did* come back. He did so after I moved from Sun City Center to a home in Virginia where I live as I write this. I am happy, but there is more to the story.

About a week after I arrived at my new home in Virginia, suddenly my earrings flew off and onto the floor in front of me. When I picked them up, the backs were still attached. This to me is a sign that my Leprechaun had returned and was trying to communicate. I had a strong feeling that he had something to do with me getting my new house. I believe this was his gift. Later I used my pendulum to ask about it. There was a very strong "yes" to the question. I tearfully thanked him and blessed him with all my heart. Then he left. He has not been back since.

III.
MOM AGAIN

Maybe as long as a year after the first Leprechaun adventure, I decided I would pay to have another session with Carl. During that session I mentioned that my mother was with me. He wanted to check something and did so. He told me that she had not yet "gone to the light" and that he knew it was important for her to do that. He asked me if I would mind if he helped her do it. I knew it was in my mother's best interest, even though I would miss her, so I said yes. He said that she could come back afterwards if she chose. So he again called in the Angels of Transition and her family and friends who had passed. Carl told me she went away slowly looking back at me, and in her eyes she was saying "are you sure that this is okay?" She looked frightened. When Carl told me that, I spoke to my mother and told her it was what was good for her, and she needed to do it. I said she could come back to me again. I was going to miss her. She went away with them. Her family members and friends were hugging her and smiling.

Later I found out that she returned to me. My friend Teri gave me another Reiki session. My mother was there, as discussed in a previous chapter. I believe she is still with me.

CHAPTER THIRTY

Energy Healing

During the past four years a great amount of information that has come my way about issues that most people would only laugh about. They have no idea that it is actually factual. Mankind has scientifically proven much. The following is a list of some of the issues and experiences that I have encountered. In this chapter, I will discuss healing. I feel I have healed myself, and others. (Remember the dental experience and the chapter about prayer). Love and belief do it. You could too. Love is the best healer of them all . . . and the best creator.

I.
CAT

I had a dangerously ill cat. He couldn't swallow food or water. I took him to the vet and discovered that he had a blockage somewhere inside him. The Vet wanted to operate, but I could not afford that, and I believed that if the cat's problem were not serious, eventually his body would heal. I would not need to spend the money. If it was serious, he might die anyway from the surgery. So, the Vet suggested I take him home and keep him in an isolated room. I needed to feed the cat food with an eyedropper and sleep with him. I was to spend lots of time with him and give him affection. When I slept on the bed with him, I decided to send love into his body. I closed my eyes and pictured God sending love through me into the cat. I fed him with the eyedropper as instructed.

We spent several days in "medical mode" until my dear friend was able to eat and drink by himself.

At that point I took him back to the vet. I told them what I had done and added that I loved him into wellness. I was told that they were not surprised that I could heal him with love, since this type of healing has worked before. Love *can* heal. Just believe!

I guess Veterinarians and Dentists have seen some interesting things in their years of experience. I call what I did "Reiki". I believe it is another word for Love Healing. I wonder if Jesus did this type of healing. If God is indeed Love, *He* is surely involved.

II.
CHILD

One of my art students, a young lady, had a headache one day during her lesson. She happened to mention it. I had a feeling I could fix her problem and I asked her if I could try something. Maybe I could help. She said "okay". I put my hands on her head and asked God's permission to help her. I got a feeling of yes and pictured God sending his love through me, into my hands, then into her head. In about one minute she said the headache was gone.

III.
TADPOLES

Sometimes I can stop medical problems for only a short time. For example: I had a frog in a fish tank, which produced lots of frog eggs. When they came out of the eggs, after a few days the little tadpoles started to die in great numbers. It upset me to watch their struggle and demise. I wanted to stop this disturbing trend. I needed to do something. I did not know at the time if I even had a chance at it. But I decided to try to help anyway and put my hands on the front of the tank. I pictured sending love into the tank the way I sent love into my cat and the student in the previous examples. The next morning I saw that the tadpoles had stopped dying. Unfortunately, they only lived for another day or so. Maybe if they were in a real pond, they could have lived? I wonder.

IV.
MY OWN PAIN

I listened to a book once on tape, which was sent to me by a close friend. The title was *Mutant Message Down Under*, written by Marlo Morgan. Ms. Morgan "calls it" fiction. Some of the happenings in that book inspired and intrigued me. During the interaction with the aborigine people in that book, she discusses how she was shown the process, which their "medical person" used to heal a badly broken bone. There was an amazing healing and the person could walk on that leg the next day. Part of the procedure was stroking the damaged leg gently and speaking lovingly, asking the leg to remember how it was before the injury. Since then I have attempted to heal some of my own medical problems in this way. It has worked.

I tried it when I stubbed my toe badly attempting to get into the shower and when my finger hurt one morning with no apparent reason. Both times I stroked the area involved very gently and lovingly and told it that I loved it. I asked it to remember what it was like before the incident that gave it pain and go back to that state of being. Perhaps it was the "mustard seed of belief" that made it possible, but the pain ended within a minute. I suspect that our bodies are more conscious than we think, and will do whatever it takes to protect us, as in the chapter about the Firewalk.

Nature's mysteries keep being revealed as needed. Just BELIEVE.

CHAPTER THIRTY-ONE

Aura Photography

For many years now I have been attending a "Coptic Conference" with friends from the Metaphysical Club in Florida. Carl Franklin and his wife run it. One year a man was at the conference offering Aura Photography to the participants for a fee. I signed up to get photographed. The idea has intrigued me since I was a teenager.

When it was my turn to be photographed, I walked into a room above the main event area. A man asked me to sit in front of a computer screen. He sat next to me. The machine he used was connected to the computer screen. I was able to watch the changes in my aura as I sat there. The operator took my picture at what he thought was a typical moment in the cycle of the colors. Generally my aura was a pinkish blue color with white showing up over my head. Afterwards I was given a multiple page report about the results, which included the picture of me with my aura. There was an in-depth explanation of what the colors meant, which was so very close to my personality that I could not help staring at it.

If you are unfamiliar with auras, I can tell you in my own words what I believe they represent: Our aura is our life force, our soul, which generally is not visible to us, but is that which is alive and keeps our body together. When it is gone, our body disintegrates. That force is "us". We resemble the electricity which makes our lamps light and our TV come alive just during the time it runs through. We usually can't see it, but it is there. I have heard that no one can see his or her own aura. However, I saw mine on that computer screen that day.

I believe when we are "in our bodies" this "electricity" continues on inside us, although we can't see that part. The colors of it change with our thoughts and emotions. Our aura colors can only be seen by this special machine, and the people who have learned how to "see" them. (I have met several who can do so when they can "look" in a special way). Our personality shows up in these colors too.

Because we are a form of energy we can't really die. Some people, who have had the experience of what we call death, don't even know they are dead because they still have that same consciousness. They take it with them. The body immediately starts to disintegrate without that force.

CHAPTER THIRTY-TWO

Vibrations

I.
WE ARE ONE

When I lived in New Hampshire, I was investigating different ideas and trying them out for myself. One idea was to think of the world as a whole unit and feel it, to see it in my mind. I was thinking in terms of "We are one". I was trying it in my car one day. I saw in my mind the road as it went over the horizon and all the way around the earth. I felt vibrations in my body. It was like chills or "goose bumps" but I was not cold. I found that I could make it happen. Afterwards over a series of years I was starting to feel it more easily and more often. It seemed to happen more when I was in touch with God in some way. I sense that it is part of my contact with nature too, as God and nature feel so intertwined. This effect grew to include more of my body. It eventually went down my legs. I now can feel it in my entire body when I say: "We are one".

II.
PRAYER OVER FOOD

In one book I read, *Love Without End, Jesus Speaks*, by Glenda Green, Jesus communicated that if we pray a certain way over our food, it will *change* the food. I feel that it might really be changing it at that moment. I have been using the prayer mentioned in the book on a regular basis and have found that the same vibrations I have been feeling in the above

"We Are One" experience also are felt when I use this prayer. However, I have to be feeling the presence of God and speaking directly to Him *sincerely* when this occurs. I stare at the food as I'm speaking and it seems to be in some way "more alive". It shines.

If this idea intrigues you, here is the prayer that I use:

> *"Bless this food Oh Lord I pray, make it become exactly what my body needs by the time it gets in there today. Bless all those who made it possible to nourish myself with it and thank you, God, for providing for me with this food. I am blessed. Amen."*

I believe that it must have almost this exact wording. All three parts are important: Blessing the food, blessing those who made it possible to nourish ourselves with it, and thanking God. Thanking God seems to cause the most vibration. I suspect you can add anything you like to these words if it comes from your heart. You could even name those who grew the food, those who became the food, prepared the food, etc. (Even just saying this to myself as I write, I have those vibrations).

Truly God is all around us if we pay attention.

GOD BEHIND ME

God behind me, God before me,
God beside me, God within,
No matter what befalls me,
I know that I'm with Him.

CHAPTER THIRTY-THREE

Animal Communication

I.
USING YOUR HEART

This is about knowing in your heart that other forms of life are really just like us on the inside. They have a life. They communicate with their fellows and have children. They may do it in a different way than we do, but they love, and grow, and feel and learn. They may see things a little differently. They may actually love better than humans do. Plant, animal, bug or human, this is about looking into the eyes of another creature and seeing their soul. This is about caring. This is about joining someone else in *their* world. Historically, humans have had a hard time doing that. They seem to even have a hard time doing that with their own species! In the not to distant future, we may need to learn how to accept, love and understand other forms of life – even from other planets. Will we be ready? I hope so. Can we see love in the eyes of another, no matter what shape they hold? Why not look for it! You might get a blessing you didn't expect!

II.
CATS

As a child, I had a series of cats. My parents observed that I was gentle with them when they took me to visit someone with kittens. They gave me a cat for Christmas the follow year. I was five.

Years later, with one of these wonderful furry friends, I used to sit down near the heat vent in the winter. I was sensitive to the cold among other things, so I spent a lot of time there. At this time I decided to try mental telepathy, which I had recently heard about, in order to see if it was truly possible. The cat was a convenient trial animal. When the cat got off my lap and walked away, I decided to try sending a loving message to him. I stared at his head as he sat facing the opposite way from me, and I spoke in my mind as I focused on his head and thought, "I love you very much". I said it in my mind and with feeling. His ears turned back. I was awed. I saw that as possible proof that it worked. I have tried it again after that with other cats and it still works.

III.
LIZARD

In my work life I was an Administrative Assistant at various companies. In one office in the 2001 there was a co-worker who decided to keep a fish tank on his desk with a lizard in it. He left it there during the weekends. I felt that it was a mistake to do so because the building temperature was much lower. The lizard would need to be warmer. I was concerned.

One day I decided to go over and check on the lizard when his owner was away from his desk. I looked into the eyes of the lizard and spoke to him. "I hope you are okay. Are you warm enough?" In the eyes of the lizard there was terrible suffering. I knew he was going to die. The sadness broke my heart. I wanted so very much to help him. All I could do was to blow warm air into the cage. I knew it was not enough. I also knew that the owner would not believe me that his pet needed help, nor would he care very much if the poor thing died. The next day, the lizard was dead. I grieved. A dear friend had passed away. I felt I was the only one who actually cared. I was certainly the only one who really knew this beautiful soul. I had seen it in his eyes.

IV.
SNAKES A

Most people are afraid of snakes. I am not. When I was a child I watched a show on television about handling snakes. I was interested in how the handlers were working with them. I decided that I would go out to the park and see if I could find one. Fortunately, I did not find one. However, the seed was planted.

As an adult many years later, I have encountered several snakes. I am cautious, but not really afraid. I speak to them. I feel like they listen to the inflections in my voice and know my intentions.

One day I was walking down a path in the woods around Kenoza Lake in Massachusetts. There was a black snake on the side of the path. I stopped and spoke to it. I looked him in the eye and said hello. I told him that I hoped he was having a nice day. I was sincere. I walked on, but looked back at him and I saw him suddenly turn and put his head up to see me in what I think was a stare of surprise. No other human probably ever gave him that simple kindness. I would react similarly if I were he. I felt his perplexity and awe.

V.
SNAKES B

When I moved to Virginia, one of my daughters came for a short visit with my grandson. During that visit a snake appeared in my home. My twelve-year old grandson discovered it. He came to me and told me that there was a snake curled up by a wall in the basement near where he had planned to sleep that night. (He changed his sleeping arrangements afterward). I went down to find a colorful, and probably poisonous, snake curled up in a resting mode. I spoke to it and told it that it did not belong inside the house since there would be no food for him. I would happily help him to get back outdoors.

I found a cardboard box and carefully placed it over the snake telling him. "You will be okay. I will not hurt you". I put a piece of flat cardboard under him and the box. Then I carried him outside to a wooded spot. When I lifted the box off, he looked at me a moment and slithered away. He looked directly at me. He did not seem angry.

VI.
SNAKES C

After my daughter and grandson left, I discovered another snake, also poisonous, in front of the front door, which was open. I have a storm door also, and it was closed. I looked at the snake and gently told him that he did not belong inside as there was no food for him, and he needed to go out the door. I opened the storm door, told him to go on out, making a swishing movement toward the door with the other hand. He looked at me and slithered outside disappearing under the porch. I believe at this point that animals of all kinds can sense your feelings. If you are afraid, they become afraid of you. Many will try to defend themselves. I believe it is important to relax and put your self in their place.

VII.
VULTURES

In Florida I spent many hours in parks. I was looking for butterflies or anything that was alive and interesting. One day I as I walked along on a trail, not finding much to photograph and was getting discouraged. Suddenly I saw two turkey vultures. I believe these were a male and female pair. I wanted to take their picture, but was unsure if they were amenable to it. I carefully walked closer till they could hear me asking if I could take their picture. I told them I would be honored if they would let me do so. I also mentioned that I thought they were quite interesting and beautiful. I continued to observe and discuss how they had pretty wings. I told them that they were amazing and wonderful creatures and that I wanted other people to properly appreciate them. From their actions, they seemed to be surprised and delighted. They posed in different positions and seemed to commiserate on the wonder of any human who would actually *like* them.

I spent about 15 minutes with them showing off for me. They opened their wings and turned to show me how they looked from the back and from the front. They showed off all their glory. When we seemed to be done, I thanked them and told them I would show others how wonderful they were. I left feeling I had made a couple of new friends who were kind and interesting, not to mention humorous.

VIII.
INSECTS

As I mentioned earlier, when I was a child, my father gave me a poetry book. The title of the book was *Favorite Poems Old and New*, by Helen Ferris. I didn't know much about poetry. I was very surprised to receive it. However, I grew to love that book. One of the poems in the book was entitled "Little Talk" by Aileen Fisher. It taught me respect for all forms of life. It talked about the possibility that insects just may talk to each other like we do. They may discuss the weather etc., but we are just too big to hear such small talk.

Also in that book: was a quote from:
The Rime of the Ancient Mariner, by Samuel
Taylor Coleridge who wrote this:

HE PRAYETH BEST

He prayeth best, who loveth best
All things both great and small;
For the dear God who loveth us,
He made and loveth all.

These poems impacted me and became a part of who I am. Perhaps it is the reason for some of the following experiences.

IX.
ANTS AND CRICKETS

I had a friend that owned a small cabin in the lakes region of New Hampshire and I was invited up to see it one day. The cabin was on a small lake and surrounded completely by woods. During that visit I was left alone for a while which I did not mind.

It was the kind of day that most people long for, a day when the temperature was perfect. A soft wind was blowing the leaves of the trees and the light was flickering through the foliage around me. There was not a human being in sight. The birds sang and flew from tree to tree as I crouched on the ground among the grasses and wild flowers. I closed my eyes and breathed in the beauty of this natural setting. I heard the lake water lapping the shore in the distance.

After a few minutes taking in the scene and feeling at total peace, I looked down and spied an ant walking up a blade of grass. I followed his progress till he came to another blade of grass and walked across it to a stalk of some wild plant. Suddenly, I was reminded of being a young girl playing on a jungle gym. I thought it would be fun to be the size of that ant and play all day on that wild "jungle gym". I smiled. Peace engulfed me. I don't know how long I stayed in that position "playing" in my mind on those blades of grass. I do know that I felt a connection to that ant, my companion in my mind in this natural playground.

Eventurally, when I raised myself from the earth, I walked slowly, attempting to hold onto the "magic" of that experience. I walked over to the cabin overlooking the lake where the trees almost obscured the site of the water. I sat on the wooden farmer's porch with my feet dangling down for a few minutes, then lay back down and closed my eyes to savor the feeling of wonder.

Eventually I opened my eyes to a movement beside me. Something small was making its way towards me. At first I was startled not knowing if it might be a bee or wasp. I "froze". At second glance I relaxed. It was only a cricket. I smiled at my silly concern. The cricket came closer and I was finally eye to eye with it, since I was back in my reclining position. We looked at each other and I could see that he was directly looking into my eyes. It seemed only polite to greet him so I said, "Well, hello! How are you today? I hope you are enjoying this lovely day". He stopped immediately. I continued to speak to him, wishing him well and discussing this and that. When I could think of no more "small talk", I said "Well that is about all for now. I think I will rest". I started to turn away and I saw him continue his walk along the edge of the porch till he was out of view.

After a little more relaxation on the porch, I decided to see what was on the side of the house. Perhaps there would be flowers. I ambled to the side of the house and looked around. I tried to sit down, but it was uncomfortable in that location. As I was trying to figure out what to do next, I noticed a movement in the grass. As I looked more closely I could see that it was a cricket. It seemed identical to the one who I had met earlier. I said to myself "Could it be him?" I was curious and moved closer to ask him if he was the same one. As soon as the words were out of my mouth, this little "friend" leaped at me and landed on the front of my shirt. His behavior was so unexpected that I jumped and knocked him off. I didn't mean to do that.

When I realized what I had done, I felt guilty for my inappropriate behavior and apologized. I said, "I am so sorry. You surprised me. I didn't mean to harm you. I love you. Please forgive me. I guess it would be a good idea if you didn't jump on humans. They are too nervous around such as you". He stayed where he was after that and I spoke to him a moment more. We parted and I went about my human business, and he went about his own "cricket business".

X.
DRAGONFLIES

In my adventures with butterfly photography, I have often come upon dragonflies. I have observed hundreds of them over the years. I have found them to be friendly creatures. They have "posed" for their pictures at my entreaties. I always tell them how beautiful I find them to be (and mean it), and that I want other humans to properly appreciate them. I tell them it is the reason why I want to take their picture.

On one occasion I met several dragonflies on a hike in the woods. I had been "having problems" with mosquitoes. It occurred to me that it would be to our mutual advantage to continue on the path together. I spoke to my new friends about it. I mentioned that they could have great meal opportunities, and I could be saved from those pests. It was perfect for us both. To my surprise and delight, my new friends proceeded to follow me as far as I went on the trail. No mosquitoes bit me during that time. What a deal!

It sure is great to have the right friends show up at the right time. They blessed my life that day.

CHAPTER THIRTY-FOUR

Tree Communication

I.
NEW HAMPSHIRE

On one of my many adventures climbing my favorite mountain in New Hampshire, I stopped to check out a tree that grew along the side of the trail. I had gotten into the habit of hugging trees (I guess that makes me an official "tree hugger") from time to time, and I felt sorry for this particular tree. It was damaged. I hugged it, and while I was doing so, I put my head on it and closed my eyes. To my surprise, while my eyes were closed, I began to "see" a distorted picture of a forest that was similar to the area where the tree grew. It seemed ethereal. This viewing lasted as long as my eyes were closed, in this case about a minute. This has never happened before or since.

My version of what I was seeing is the following: The tree was grateful for my affectionate behavior and gave me the gift of how it "saw" the environment where it was living. This brings to mind that I have read in several books that all things have consciousness. Trees are no exception.

II.
FLORIDA

Also, during the time I lived in Florida, I had another experience of communication with a tree. This occurred while I went for a walk with a friend. During the walk we were coming up to a very large oak. I was impressed with it. I spoke to the tree telling it how I respected and loved it for all it did. I mentioned how it gave homes to many forms of life and how it gave humans shade from the sun, and oxygen for us to breathe. I had a longer list, which I shared with the tree. Then I told it that I wished it well and blessed it.

I walked on down the street with my friend. We were talking as we ambled on. Around the corner, but still within view, I felt something hit my back enough to definitely get my attention. It did not feel like a person touched me. It was not my friend Rose. It felt like energy or concentrated wind. I turned around. I could still see the tree behind me in the distance. Some part of me *knew* it was that tree. I believe that it was saying thanks in its own way.

NATURE'S CALL

There's magic in the wind
As it moves among the trees.
There's music in the forest
With bird song on the breeze.
I can hear the gentle murmur
Of the voice of nature say –
Come hear me, see me, know me,
And be with me today.

CHAPTER THIRTY-FIVE

Jesus Heals

This is a recent "special" experience. It occurred during the preparations to publish *A List of "Miracles" and Daring to Tell*. It involved my friend Jeanette who gave me permission to include the facts about our joint experiences with Jesus.

It all began with a difficult and upsetting experience I had at home. I was overwhelmed with emotional distress and was trying hard to get past it. I felt strongly that I would need some extra help and asked Jesus for that help. I somehow "knew" that Jesus came and stood by my bed. He tried to console me, and he held my hand for a few minutes. He said some things to me that I now cannot remember. But I felt very blessed by his presence and his help.

When I started to feel better, I remember asking him if he would please go help my dear friend Jeanette who was very ill. I told him that I would miss him, but she needed him more. Then I thought to myself that maybe it would be handy if he could be in more than one place at a time. He piped up and said the word "bi-location". Then I remembered reading about this ability of his in a book entitled *Anna, Grandmother of Jesus*, by Claire Heartsong, and I knew he could, and probably would, do it. I verified it with him. I was intensely grateful, as I was extremely concerned. I felt strongly that if anyone could help her, it would be Jesus. Then he left the room.

A few minutes after he left, it dawned on me that it might be good to let my friend know that she would probably get a visit soon. It might encourage her. I called her and explained what had just occurred. I mentioned that Jesus might very well show up to help her. She seemed happy and hopeful.

A week or more later, I got a call from Jeanette who was extremely excited. She told me that she had just had a special Reiki healing session with a Teri Taylor, a Reiki Practitioner of many years experience and a dear friend of mine. Jeanette said she could hardly believe what happened. She was in awe. Near the beginning of the Reiki session, Teri suddenly stopped and said that she noticed that suddenly someone came to help that had never shown up before in her work. . She said that Jesus appeared and started to help with the healing. He moved all around my friend healing different parts of her body.

At the end of the session, both of the women told Jesus they were honored by his presence and his help. Then Jesus surprised them both. He told them, (in my words), that he was also honored to be working with them. Below is a quote from an e-mail that was sent to me by the Reiki practitioner about the incident.

> "Did Jeanette tell you that I did REIKI on her last weekend, and the spirit of Jesus came in and assisted in the healing? I have never had that happen before, and at session's end, she told me that you had recently made contact with Jesus and had asked him to help her. Isn't that incredible!" We were both very honored.

Jeanette sent me the following excerpt from her journal about the experience and allowed me to add it here. Please note that I have removed some of the statements which are not relevant and which are also personal. Where information has been removed you will see "..."

Sat. 6-4-11 Reiki Reading with Teri Taylor

Today's session was so amazing, I don't know where to begin . . .

. . . At the beginning of the session Teri got the word quiet...She said this was going to be a quiet session. . . .

. . . .Teri then said she saw Golden Light pouring into the area of my body where the energy stone was laying, Then Teri said, "I see many beams of golden light pouring down on your body and spreading light beams out from the energy stone all over and enfolding your entire body, "They're infusing you with healing." Then Teri said, "This light is Christ Light."

Then Teri paused for a moment, and hesitantly stated, "Nothing like this has ever happened before, in these sessions, but I think the spirit of Jesus is here." She said, "He is standing across from me." She said His energy was absolutely "peaceful and loving." She said that he began working on the right side of my body. Teri told me that He said that He was aware of my suffering and that I was not alone. *I then became filled with peace and stillness. Teri observed him placing his hands all around my body with a gentle and loving touch... what I felt was peace just peace, and sweet energy. Intuitively I knew I was healed at all levels of my being. He paid special attention to placing his hands under my body where I had been experiencing such pain sitting. Because I brought up my issue of having a balance disorder, He moved around to my head and placed his hands on top of my head and held them there for some time.*

I then had a thought in my mind that I would like Teri to be acknowledged. In an instant Teri said to Jesus that it was an honor that he had come. In turn Jesus said that it was His honor to see we two girls who cared about each other working together in the light.

Jesus remained there with us the entire 1-hour session. When he left, he kissed me on the right cheek.

After our session Teri said that I was being filled with the Golden Light energy the entire session. Teri was quite surprised when I told her that Jesus visited our mutual friend, Elizabeth, a few weeks ago. She had a conversation with Him and as part of the conversation she asked Jesus if he would visit me, as I was having serious medical problems. Knowing that, I began praying to Jesus letting him know that I was open and ready to receive His presence.

This was by far the best Reiki session I have ever experienced... hands down! Jesus came!!!...Stayed the whole session, OMG! He brought me peace and stillness.

And to think Jesus was honoring us.

It's difficult for me to absorb it all right now, as I am stunned!

(End of Journal Entry)

As you can see, I am not alone in having "miracles" in my life. This was a significant experience for the three of us (Teri, Jeanette and me), and it also proves the love that Jesus has for those who believe in him, not to mention what he has done for all of humanity. The words "Jesus Cares" suddenly has taken on additional meaning for us.

CHAPTER THIRTY-SIX

The Fountain of Youth

Back in the later part of the 1980's I received a book from my brother for Christmas. It was unusual for him to give me a gift. I knew that it was an indication of his respect for the information therein. I was curious. The title of the book was *Ancient Secret of the Fountain of Youth* by Peter Kelder.

When I first opened the book, I read the comments by those who had read it before me. I read: "I got my hair back", "I feel great", "I am full of energy." etc. The readers painted a rosy picture. I continued on and found a very interesting story. It told of two men who were friends. One left to go abroad and came back many years later. When they met again the man who had left looked younger than when he had departed on his journey. The bottom line was that he had learned how to make himself have a younger looking body. He shared the "secret" with his companion who eventually wrote the book, which includes what *I* have called "exercises". In the book they are called "The Rites". These movements are based on Hatha Yoga according to the author.

I have been doing these "Rites" for a good twenty years or more. People say I look younger than my age. One person did not believe me when I told him how old I was and asked to look at my driver's license. I have been quite healthy. I have had noticeably less health issues. I quit going to doctors. I no longer feel so depressed. I don't use prescription drugs or any other kind of drugs. I *do* take over the counter vitamins and pills with black cohash to deal with the inconveniences of menopause. I do not have a problem with my weight. If I start to gain weight, I control my intake of food immediately. People say I am thin.

Interestingly perhaps, I *don't* do all the Rites that they recommend. I do only one half as many. They still have helped me.

I know that if I stop doing these rites for two or more days, I feel desperately upset and anxious. I have even felt suicidal. I no longer allow myself to stop the exercises for that long. No matter what happens, I am strongly determined to continue. The book warns the reader that if you want to stop doing the Rites, you must back off slowly. When I broke my arm in 2003, I did my best to keep up my regime.

These rites include five types of movements. The reader is asked to do each one the same number of times, doing them in the correct order, and you must start with no more than three of each and do them for at least a week before adding two more of each to the regimen, then two each week thereafter till a total of 21 of each is reached, which is recommended as a final goal.

I found out some interesting information about these Rites. First, the author said the information came from the famed monks in Tibet. The other is that these Rites help to balance what some call our chakras. Doctors have called these our "glands".

If these rites interest you, and you would like to read up on them, the books are available at Barnes and Noble. There are now two books. Book II gives more detail about the rites and includes other information regarding the source of the rites. Even if you don't want to check out the book to do these rites, you may find the information intriguing.

CHAPTER THIRTY-SEVEN

Grandparent Update

On July 17th 2011, I went to bed at night and lay there reading for a while. Eventually, I put the book aside and for some unknown reason began thinking of my Grandfather. I wondered for the first time if he had followed the light to "heaven" or if he just stayed here as my mother had done. I suspected that he had not completed the process and gone where he was supposed to go. I believed that he could not leave me. He knew I needed him. I knew he had been with me for many years, probably since he "transitioned".

As I had often done in the past, I decided to talk to my Grandfather. I "knew" where he was in the room. I looked that way, and explained that I felt he needed to go if he had not followed the light already. I told him that he would be able to return if he chose, and I would be totally delighted to have him join me again after he found his way there. I told him he could call in the Angel/s of Transition to assist him in finding his way. Also, I asked the Angels of Transition to help him. Then I asked for those who he knew and loved from the other side to come and get him. They did. I sensed that he was gone for a few minutes.

As I expected, he returned. Even though my eyes could not see him, my heart could, and I gave him a big hug (in the air) with tears in my eyes. That hug was returned with great love and feeling, I could tell. My heart could feel that hug. I told him how happy I was that he had spent so many years with me, and told him how much he meant to me. I expressed to him how grateful I was that he had returned.

Very shortly afterward, something told me somehow that my Grandfather had brought my Grandmother back with him. She was standing right next to him. I reached out my hands to hers and we held hands for a while (also in the air). A warm feeling of love washed over me and I knew it was returned. A couple of minutes later I just jumped out of bed and started writing so that I would not forget one piece of what I experienced. They were still there as I wrote this.

My gratefulness and love for these two wonderful people is hard to express. I am grateful to God also that I can sense their presence and their love.

A love expressed and returned
Is never forgotten.
Though unseen by human eyes,
Love never dies.

CHAPTER THIRTY-EIGHT

Jesus Returns

On July 16, 2011, several weeks after the "Jesus Healing" experience, I received a call from Jeanette again. Jesus had returned at *another* session with Teri Taylor. She asked if I wanted to continue putting the information in my book. I told her that I believe it is part of the on-going saga of "miracles". Indeed, she felt she had seen a group of "miracles" since Jesus had come the first time. Jeanette said she would provide additions to her journal so that I could share what happened. She also asked if I would contact another person to procure his approval to use his name, which I did. He had been responsible for what she believed was another miracle. I received the fastest reply possible. It was almost instantaneous. That alone seemed like a miracle, but I have heard, read and experienced that there are "no coincidences". (I reluctantly did not actually use that information in this writing however, since the subject of this chapter was relating only to Jesus.)

The following are excerpts from Jeanette's journal regarding the "second coming" of Jesus to her healing session. Again I have removed the personal information and where this takes place I have put in the same notations as the last adventure with Jesus.

6-11-11 *Journal Entry*
Here it is a week later. I am writing in my journal still incredibly in awe that Jesus came to me.

Looking back, my friend Elizabeth was visited by Jesus a few weeks ago she had a conversation with Him and as part of the conversation she asked Jesus if he would visit me as I was having serious health problems. Afterward Elizabeth let me know she had requested Jesus visit me. I was prompted to pray to Jesus, in an effort to make it clear to Him that I was open and very willing to receive His presence.

I didn't get off my now so sacred massage table 100% healed, rather it has been a beautiful process of unfolding changes with information coming to me as needed for my healing. My intuition has graduated to quite keen!

Subsequent to that visit on 6-4-11, I have noticed that day-by-day my strength is increasing and Healing miracles began to unfold in my life . . .

JUNE 23 JOURNAL ENTRY

Since Jesus visited me, I have had clarity about my healing needs and Miracles almost daily bringing knowledge and use of the newest innovative healing methods and protocols, which are useful and effective . . . always orchestrated by my spirit family... Praise God!!!

7-16-11 JOURNAL ENTRY REIKI SESSION WITH TERI TAYLOR.

When Teri arrived for our session, she excitedly reported about the messages she received in transit: . . .

. . . Lo and behold, the next thing happening is Teri announcing, "JESUS is here!!!!" Oh my goodness, my emotions began doing cartwheels! I was repeating myself. Jesus is here? Jesus is here? In my fondest dreams, I did not expect Jesus to visit again. Teri reported to me that

Jesus positioned himself at my head. Next thing, Teri said. "I can feel him entering my body." She became the embodiment of Christ energy. Jesus now with his hands on my shoulders and Teri working on my head to clear out the "clutter" of my overly busy mind. Working at my temples and crown... Teri felt Jesus directing and assisting her hands, working as he was outside and inside her body, which I'll call a local bi-location. Jesus said this is a "twofer." I asked what was a twofer? He said the session was a two-for-one. Jesus definitely does not lack a sense of humor! Jesus said that he concurred with and encouraged me to follow the advice Teri's guides had given her and emphasis was reinforced: . . .

Our session ended 1-1/2 hour later with Teri and I expressing our profound appreciation and gratitude.

(End of Journal Entry)

COURAGE

T'is the courage to try
When your world falls in –
To look to the sky
In your human skin,
The world to see
In it's good and bad,
And be willing to face
The tragic and sad . . .
To be happy with you,
When others cause pain,
To be able to see
Beyond the rain -
The truth to pursue
When others deny,
It takes a special
Heart to try.

CHAPTER THIRTY-NINE

Protection

I.
THERE IS HELP

There are occasional times in life, from my experience, when we needed serious help or protection. For most of my life I didn't know anyone who could help me. Included below are a few of those moments when I had to solve the problems myself and some events when I asked for help from unseen angels and got it.

When I met Carl Franklin, I found out that there *was* help out there and that I could ask for it. Besides my friend Carl and his wife, in my case, I found out we each have a "team" of angels assigned to us. We can ask them for help. They cannot intervene unless we ask. (However, they will help without us asking if our lives are in danger and it is not our time to go, as I found out and mentioned in an earlier chapter).

Other people we come in contact with have problems sometimes, and we may want to help them. There have also been times when I thought other people were acting strangely. Mostly this strange behavior was illogical, but also negative or fearful. The good news is that it may be possible to help them. There are also special Angels who can assist us when we have a serious challenge and we need someone who can fight for us. Jesus can also help, and I am one of many who have received that kind of blessing.

The following information is about my "adventures" with situations that I have encountered and was able to either help myself or someone else through requesting assistance from the Angels and/or Jesus.

II.
UNKNOWN VISITOR/A CLOSE ENCOUNTER

When I lived in New Hampshire after the divorce, I had a visitor one night that showed up as a large black being that was taller than me. I was in my bedroom when I saw him. He had dark robes and I could feel the negative energy of this being. I could feel that he was trying to scare me. At first it was successful, but I figured out a way to get around this guy, and the trouble he was trying to cause.

After about a minute of shock, I addressed this entity. I said something like this: "I know that you are trying to scare me, but I really think you would be better off if you didn't try to run around scaring people, but instead could be open to love and friendship. I doubt you have ever had any love in your life before this, but I know you would be a lot more comfortable and joyful if you allowed it into your life. Believe me. You would be so very much happier if you did. I can be a great friend. I think you would enjoy my friendship a lot more. I am a very loving person". I was sincere. I think he knew it. He left. I guess he didn't want to be loved?

III.
ANOTHER VISITOR

I went to visit my brother and his wife who lived and worked in the Philadelphia area. They had rented a house owned by an artist and they thought it would be nice for me to see it. Thanksgiving was also a good excuse for visiting them. I came to celebrate. They asked me if I could stay for the weekend. I agreed.

They gave me a room off the basement, which the owner of the home had used for teaching art. It was a very nice looking room and comfortable. However, it did not stay that way for long.

I can't remember whether it was morning or night that I suddenly felt a body climbing onto the bed next to me, then over me to the other side. It put itself against me at my back. I could not see it, *but felt it physically.* I knew it was trying to scare me. It succeeded in doing so. However, this event was after the other one that I mentioned, *and learned from.* Again I tried to get out of my trouble by suggesting warmth and friendship. Before long it was gone.

IV.
HELPING OTHERS

In the last five years, I have had some challenging situations with other people. I could tell these people were acting in strange and negative ways. They were based in fear.

The first time I encountered a situation like that I had the occasion to ask for help from Carl Franklin. I was just having a "normal" conversation and happened to bring up the fact that I was afraid to return to the New Hampshire apartment where I took my vacations due to a man there with whom I did not want to come in contact. He asked me to tell him the details, so I did. He said he could help me.

He "checked" to see something first, and then told me that the man had three "entities" attached to him and they were causing him to act those strange ways. They were negative beings. He said he could remove them. Before he "cleared" them, he told me that *I* would have to commit to protecting this man, twice a day for a month.

Carl had already suggested the year before, that I would benefit myself by asking my personal team of Angels and Guides to help me by surrounding me in a "Protective Bubble of Divine Love and Light where only Love can enter and only Love may stay" every day, in the morning (to last till evening) and then the evening (to last till morning). This is the prayer I use often, but I also *picture* this happening for myself at times.

In this new situation, I was to picture this bubble of Devine Love and Light surrounding my New Hampshire neighbor for five minutes straight in the morning and the same in the evening. This was to make sure that the entities did not return. Carl said to check with him after a month was over. He would see if it worked.

I agreed to be responsible to keep these "entities" at bay and make sure they would not return. He removed them by calling in the Angels of Transition, etc. Then, since they would not leave, he had to call in Arch Angel Michael to take them away. That worked. Then it was my turn.

Every day for a month I "put" a bubble of Divine Love and Light around my neighbor at the appropriate times each day for five minutes. It took some serious concentration to do so and sometimes I felt like I was fighting something to do it. I believe I probably *was* fighting those entities. I also "felt" the joy of the neighbor when I extended the "Bubble" out from him as far as the street on one occasion. I could tell it was an enormous relief to him to be free of those beings, although he did not realize what was *really* happening. He was just happy.

When the month had concluded, I called Carl to ask if the plan had worked. The answer was "yes". I was relieved and wondered how it would affect the behavior of my neighbor. When I next went up to New Hampshire, I could tell a difference. He was not so aggressive.

I also had another occasion later where a clearing of entities was necessary. This person had nine of them to be removed. I was told to do the same procedure for *three* months after the clearing. That worked also according to Carl. The person changed greatly afterwards.

Per Carl Franklin, it is very important never to divulge to the person who has entities, what is going on, and that you are doing anything about it. However, it is a relief to know that one can correct a situation like that. He did not explain why I was not supposed to tell "the subject" with the problem about it, but I can imagine it would cause an almost impossible situation trying to fight these entities from coming back.

V.
BAD DREAM?

When I lived in Florida, I worked as a Care Giver for several people. One of them was an especially dear lady to me, who has now passed on "to her reward". During the time I worked for her, I was asked to live with her for two weeks as she had just come home from a hospital stay. I agreed.

I had some reservations about staying there due to a sense that there was one or more negative "spirits" in her home making sure she was not well. I often tried to surround her with a bubble of Divine Love and Light to protect her. I was not totally sure that those beings were there. In any event, I packed up my things, drove to her home and made myself as comfortable as possible in her extra bedroom for the two weeks as expected.

After I had been at her home for a few days, I experienced a very disturbing "dream" early in the morning. Some kind of negative entity, who looked like a man, attacked me and held me in a tight grip holding me from behind. He had some kind of weapon, possibly a knife that he pushed into my back a little at a time. It was extremely painful. I had no idea why he was doing it. In my pain and confusion I enquired why he was doing this. He did not reply, but looked at me with an evil smile and pushed the projectile further into my back.

I fortunately awoke at that point and escaped any more pain. However, I was quite terrified and wanted to stay awake so as not to repeat the experience. It was difficult. A memory came at that point (from where

I can only guess), that I could call on Arch Angel Michael, and perhaps Jesus as well, to help me. I needed the BIG BOYS! So I prayed to them to help me keep this "thing" at bay, even if it *was* a dream. I asked them to protect me and to keep the house safe at least as long as I was staying there, and if possible, longer for the sake of that dear lady. I could picture them arriving and doing the job. I felt safer and had no more nightmares in her home.

It would seem to me, from my own experience, that I have truly been assisted by Jesus and the Angels. I am deeply grateful for their valuable assistance. I also know that those I count on for help love *you* too, and would do the same for you if you asked. In your times of trial, may you be blessed also by the assistance of these special and loving "beings".

THANK YOU

Thank you for your counsel, dearest friends.
You were there when need turned into pain
To show me all the things I could not see,
You helped me learn to fight my fight again.

CHAPTER FORTY

A Leap of Faith

The first big leap of faith I managed to accomplish was the decision to get a divorce back in 1985. I thought that I would end up in a rat-infested apartment in which my children and I would end up starving. It would have been just barely better than suicide. But I had a conversation with God as part of that decision. He asked me one question: "Who do you love more, your husband or me?" I said "you God".

I left the church where that conversation took place and went straight to a lawyer who explained what things would look like afterward. He gave me peace enough to change my life. I was still terrified, but I knew if God was involved, somehow it would turn out for the best.

Many years later, having lived in Florida to take care of my parents, I wanted to leave when that part of my life was concluded. During the time I was there, I watched as both of my parents died. It was a very difficult part of my life. I felt almost desperate to return to New Hampshire afterward. However, I had bought a home in Florida and had lived in it less than two years. I wanted to wait till the two years had been completed before I sold my home. I wanted to avoid giving any money to "Uncle Sam". I put my house up for sale anyway and waited. I started to get some interest, but I wanted to get more money, which I thought might be forthcoming. I changed the sale price up, (unfortunately a mistake). Then I simply went on vacation to New Hampshire and looked for housing.

Just as I was getting close to working everything out, the housing market took one of the biggest dives of all time. My home's value plummeted. My real estate representative suggested I take my home off the market and wait till better times. I did that.

I waited for about three years and put my home back on the market even though the value had not gone back up. I had a strong sense that I *must* leave. It no longer mattered how I did it. I lowered the price of my home to about half the price I had paid for it, which was lower than any other home of its type. I did not know how I was going to get another home anywhere for that amount, but I felt that God wanted me out of Florida. I needed to take a "Leap of Faith".

I had many friends who did not want me to go. Several people who were very important to me were angry at the thought that I would leave them. I felt however, that I would actually die if I did not leave Florida soon. I cannot explain that feeling, but it was very real to me and very obvious. I still believe it.

For a long time I received no offers at all on my home. In that town there were many people who simply abandoned their homes in order to leave. It seemed at that point almost impossible to sell my residence.

Around that time several things happened:

1. I received an audio CD about working with the angels to find out where I would be in one year. The results indicated I would not be living in Florida at the end of that time.
2. I paid Janet Reynolds to give me a reading. She told me my home would sell soon, certainly before the end of that year, but probably much sooner. She also stated that I would live "happily ever after" in my new location.
3. Carl Franklin verified that I should go to Virginia to live - instead of New Hampshire and that I really didn't belong in Florida (to his surprise). He was concerned about things working out for me in Virginia, so he checked and found

ELIZABETH FARREL

out that I would have friends and a job and it would be a good place for me.

I "knew" that I was making the correct decision in looking for a home in Virginia even though I had never lived there and I had no relatives or friends in that state. It was a frightening idea to go to a new place where I knew no one, but it was necessary. This was going to be a "Leap of Faith" in that regard as well as financially.

My decision was also colored by driving through Virginia on my way to New Hampshire to visit my family and friends and to see my favorite haunts. The western part of Virginia reminded me of the White Mountains of New Hampshire without the severe cold and three months of snow covered landscape. The real estate taxes in the region were very low in comparison with New Hampshire, which was a relief. I was familiar with this temperate zone having lived in Maryland as a child. I could handle it and I could reach Florida and New Hampshire equally with a one-day drive, although a long one.

The biggest "Leap" was financial. I could not have done it at all without my faith in God. I knew He was blessing this move and that somehow He would find a way, though I might not know what way that was, to help me to do it in spite of the housing market issues.

I also felt that the sacrifices I had made to help my family in Florida would make a difference. I felt that God would balance my life. I had been on my version of the "Cross" and he would take me down from it and help me *live* again.

Within about a month, I received an offer on my home in Florida. The offer was lower than I thought I could handle. I did not accept it. After that couple disappeared, I felt I should have accepted it and felt sad. Shortly afterward I received another offer for about the same amount. I accepted it although it scared me. It was way too low to buy another house.

126

I was now in a position of putting my life in the hands of God. However, I figured if I have to be in the hands of someone, who is more deserving of my trust?

I went forward in hope and the knowledge that God would provide. The whole process of moving to Virginia was only possible with the help of a real estate "angel" in there who promised to be "my best friend" till I got settled in a home. She appeared just when I needed her. She was a delight. (God found a good lady to help me!)

When I bought the new home, I ended up spending more money than I expected in the deal, although I loved the home and location. I had no job and no real friends when the real estate lady "let go" of me. Faith alone kept me sane.

It was only a few weeks before the blessings started to arrive. They came in the form of a wonderful lady, and musician, who took me in tow. She and I became good friends and we started singing together. I had wished for this kind of opportunity almost as far back as I could remember. The joy of singing with her was like finding heaven. Now I am a part of a group called "The Ladies of the Lake" which include the two of us plus two more women who sing and play guitars. I am in my fondest dream.

The next blessing arrived when I was searching for a climbing rose bush. I went to every Garden Center I could find, but they did not have that type of bush. Then on my way home from another failure to find it, I passed the last garden center and decided to stop and ask them if they had one. To my amazement they not only had one, but *several* of the very bush I was looking for. Not only that, but it appeared that they needed help. I offered to help them and was soon working for a sweetheart of a boss and with a wonderful co-worker. The extra money gave me a great relief.

It was soon obvious that there were butterflies all over the Garden Center. It was perfect for me - who was called "The Butterfly Lady". The boss did not mind that I spent time taking photos of them. I now call that year "The Year of the Butterflies".

I also started to have friends in my neighborhood. Eventually I met a lady down the street who needed to move out of her home and was looking for somewhere to live. I offered to rent her my extra bedroom. She accepted, which gave me enough money to do the badly needed repairs to my new residence. She is also a wonderful, totally trustworthy lady who helps with the gardening and likes to cook.

I found the perfect people to do the jobs at my home. My new boss gave me their names. One of them has done a lot of work at my home and it feels like he and his wife are family. (They were the ones who worked on my garage.) It was interesting to find that he is the same age as my oldest daughter. I feel as though I have adopted him.

When I left Florida, I wondered if I would find any orbs in Virginia. It took a little while, but they started to show up. I saw a pink one in a photo of the back yard first, then more and more appeared, as you know now that you have read my story to this point. I feel blessed by them.

God has really come through for me and shown me that trusting Him was the best possible decision to make. Through my "leap of faith" I am now living in happiness on a wooded hillside. The "Wood Fairy" in me is *finally* at home.

LORD

I shall live within the mystery of your love,
Surrounded by magic, consumed by peace,
Needing to love, to touch, to feel,
To express, that love which only gives.

Ending Note:

I am of the belief that what we humans call "Miracles" are only natural laws that we have not yet discovered. We must only "awaken" to these. I suggest you be peaceful and use love to guide you remembering the mustard seed of faith. The loving arms of nature await you. We are all in this together - we humans and other forms of life. May we all see the truth – that we are one.

> *The soul sees more that lies beneath*
> *Than all the eyes in all the earth.*
> *Should we but look beyond what's here*
> *With our invisible soul.*
> *We are but one, between, among,*
> *With God the invisible thread,*
> *That sews us together*
> *And bonds us with love.*
> *Thus we are one - together.*

May God, Nature, and Jesus bless you too.

Elizabeth Farrel

Referenced Books
&
Recommended Reading

TITLE	AUTHOR
The Highly Sensitive Person	Elaine N. Aron. Ph.D.
Embraced by the Light	Betty Eadie
Favorite Poems Old and New	Eileen Ferris
Love Without End, Jesus Speaks	Glenda Green
Anna, Grandmother of Jesus	Claire Heartsong
Ancient Secret of the Fountain of Youth	Peter Kelder
Ancient Secret of the Fountain of Youth, Book 2	Doubleday
Mutant Message Down Under	Marlo Morgan
Life after Life	Raymond A. Moody
Second Sight	Judith Orloff
Behaving As If The God In All Life Mattered	Michaelle Small Wright